WHAT'S AGE
GOT TO DO WITH IT?

Living Your Healthiest and Happiest Life

INCLUDES
ROBIN'S
MAKEOVER
GUIDE

Robin McGraw

THOMAS NELSON
Since 1798

NASHVILLE   DALLAS   MEXICO CITY   RIO DE JANEIRO

Dedication

To every woman in the world who seeks to live with dignity and grace as the pages on the calendar turn day after day. This book and the passion with which it was written are for you.

WHAT'S AGE GOT TO DO WITH IT?

© 2008, 2010 by Robin McGraw

Published in Nashville, Tennessee, by Thomas Nelson. Thomas Nelson is a registered trademark of Thomas Nelson, Inc.

Thomas Nelson, Inc., titles may be purchased in bulk for educational, business, fund-raising, or sales promotional use. For information, please e-mail SpecialMarkets@ThomasNelson.com.

Some names and identifying details have been changed to protect the identities of those mentioned.

This publication is intended to provide authoritative information in regard to the subject matter covered. The publisher and author are not engaged in rendering medical or other professional services and do not have financial or commercial interest in any of the products, services, or professionals mentioned in this book. If you require medical advice or other expert assistance, you should seek the services of a competent professional.

This publication includes a condensed version of *Robin McGraw's Complete Makeover Guide*.

ISBN 978-1-4002-8067-4 (IE)
ISBN 978-1-4002-0215-7 (TP)

Library of Congress Cataloging-in-Publication Data

McGraw, Robin.
    What's age got to do with it? : living your healthiest and happiest life / Robin McGraw.
        p. cm.
    ISBN 978-1-4002-0214-0
    1. Middle-aged persons—Health and hygiene. 2. Physical fitness for middle-aged persons. 3. Beauty, Personal. I. Title.
RA777.5.M378 2009
613.7'044—dc22   2008044460

Printed in the United States of America

10 11 12 13 14 RRD 5 4 3 2 1

Acknowledgments

W*hat's Age Got to Do with It?* has been one of the most amazing projects of my life and has been influenced and contributed to by so many wonderful people. The privilege of writing about women's health and well-being is the culmination of a lifelong passion and pursuit, and there are so many who have contributed so much to this book.

I of course want to thank Phillip, my husband of thirty-two years, for being so supportive during the seemingly endless process of research, interviews, writing, and rewriting over the last year and a half. We spoke thirty-five years ago about "growing old together" and here we are. How much fun is this!

A special thanks also to my sons Jay and Jordan, who could've made it tough on their mother growing up in a household full of men. Watching them learn, grow, and become wonderful young men who respect women and family has been a blessing. Thanks to you boys for always believing in your mother, especially in this challenge of being an author. You two are my greatest accomplishment and greatest pride in this life.

Thanks also to my wonderful and beautiful daughter-in-law Erica for the enthusiastic support and long conversations about being a young woman and living in today's ever-changing world. I am so proud of you.

As always, a special thanks to my mother-in-law Jerry McGraw for being my greatest fan and always helping me to believe in myself as a wife, mother, and most importantly, a woman. You have always been such an inspiration.

To my sister Cindi, thank you so much for being who you are. You have shown so much grace and courage in the face of unspeakable adversity that you have helped me to keep my life in perspective and never take even one day of my life for granted.

To Brenda . . . Thank you for your loyalty.

In writing a book about women being women, I am blessed to have been surrounded by some great women friends during the writing of this book. A special thanks to my best friend, Janet, for her support and the ability to make me laugh until I cry. And a special thanks to my friends Carla Pennington and Terry Wood for supporting me and helping over the last several years to develop the message that I am so passionate to share. You are all inspirational women, mothers, and professionals. I couldn't have done it without you all.

A special thanks to the tireless and ever-excited Michele Bender. You're a woman of great talent and skill and are much appreciated.

I am grateful for the team of experts who so generously gave of their time and attention to this book and for being in my life. Thank you to Dr. Howard Liebowitz and Dr. Prudence Hall, medical directors at The Hall Center in Santa Monica, California; Robert Reames, CSCS, D, CN, RTS1, CPT, personal trainer and nutritionist; Janet Harris, renowned aesthetician and owner of the Skin Rejuvenation Center in Beverly Hills; Jim Hrncir, RPh.;

Frank Lawlis, PhD, psychologist; Matthew Vanleeuwen, renowned makeup artist; Steven "Cojo" Cojocaru, fashion expert and Red Carpet reporter; and Lucie Doughty, celebrity colorist.

Thank you also to Jan Miller and Shannon Marven, my literary agents at Dupree Miller and Associates. First, thank you for being such wonderful and supportive friends and for being the most passionate and engaged agents that any author could ever want. This book would not be a reality without you both.

And finally, thank you to Thomas Nelson Publishing. Your vision and support in the evolution of this manuscript are so above and beyond. The fact that you care so much about this book has been evident since day one. Your commitment to providing a quality message to the women of this world has challenged and inspired me.

Contents

1

What's Age
Got to Do with It?

Okay, ladies, it's time to talk. And the subject is aging. From the minute we're born, we start aging. So we have to decide how we're going to handle this. Are we going to let it happen to us? Or are we going to do what we can to feel and look our best?

I honestly believe that no matter our age, most of us want to be the healthiest and most energetic and vibrant women we can possibly be. Though it takes effort and doesn't happen by chance, you can live your healthiest and happiest life. I know this because ever since my midtwenties, I have been a champion for my health and done what it takes to feel my very best. Of course, I've got a lot of living left to do, but today at the age of fifty-five, I've experienced a lot of what most women are going through or going to go through, and I've come through it feeling fabulous.

I have always tried to live each day of my life with passion and excitement, look forward to each year, and enjoy being whatever age I am. This year, that's fifty-five years young, and I'm not shy about sharing it (but I guess you can tell that from the book cover). This surprises some people, but to me, age is just a number, and I've never lived my life by that number. How many candles you blow out on your birthday cake doesn't matter. What does matter is your attitude toward life and your choice to take the best care of yourself possible. As busy women, wives, and mothers, we often put ourselves last on our very long to-do lists; many times, we don't even make it onto those lists! We are nurturing by nature, so we work hard to meet our loved ones' needs and think that by focusing on the happiness of others, we'll be happy. But often we do this at our own expense—and that's a high price to pay.

When I was raising my two boys, Jay and Jordan, I'd work hard to fix them healthy breakfasts and dinners and pack well-balanced lunches. But there were plenty of times when my own breakfast was a slice of cake and coffee, and lunch was a bag of gummy bears eaten while driving car pool. Back then I'd never let my boys or Phillip miss a checkup at the doctor and would fight tooth and nail to get an appointment *today* if they were sick. But at times, I would think, *Can this wait?* before calling the doctor for myself. Thanks to several pivotal moments in my life, which I'll discuss later in this book, you'll see that I have worked hard to change that. But I know that I'm not alone in making my family a top priority. So many women just like me do everything to attend to and anticipate the needs of their families first, but they dismiss their own needs, be it physical, mental, or emotional.

My beloved mother, Georgia, was one of these women. At just fifty-eight years old, she died of a massive heart attack while we were talking on the phone. I believe that the number one reason she passed away when she was so young was that she did not take care of herself. She was a precious, loving woman who wanted everyone else to be happy and put her five children and husband before herself every time. We were very poor, so in her mind the thought of spending any of our family's money on herself was out of the question. That meant she did not go to the doctor for regular checkups, mammograms, or the simple blood work that would have revealed her elevated risk of a heart attack, among other things. She also had horrible allergies, but even when water was literally pouring from her eyes and her nose was red and raw, she'd put off her allergy shots until she absolutely couldn't stand it anymore.

Many of my memories of my mother are of her doing for others: cooking for our family of seven, baking our favorite cakes for our birthdays, ironing my father's shirts, leaning over her sewing machine making all of our clothes, and many years later, babysitting and doting on her grandchildren. Even her final moments on this earth were spent focusing on someone other than herself—a true symbol of exactly how she lived. I was thirty-two years old at the time, and Phillip and I had just moved into a new home. The move didn't go as smoothly as planned—a delay meant that the movers arrived after midnight and a downpour turned our houseful of boxes into a soggy, stinky mess of cardboard. Wanting to comfort me while I dug through my water-logged belongings, my mother baked me a pumpkin pie. And that was the last thing she did before she died. Imagine, she was dying from a heart attack and there she was rolling out pie dough! More than two decades later, the thought of that still gives me a lump in my throat and brings tears to my eyes. I admire and try to emulate an endless number of my mother's qualities, like her Christian faith, her fierce love for her family, and her strength during difficult times, but her decision to neglect herself is not one of them. From the day she died, I vowed not to continue the legacy of self-neglect.

As a result, I have made it one of my life's missions to achieve and maintain the best state of health I possibly can. It has become a passion, hobby, and commitment that has often involved hours a day scouring the Internet, reading books, and interviewing experts to learn everything I can about women's health. My goal has always been to find every tool possible to influence the pace with which I age and discover the best way to do it with grace. But that day my mother died, I didn't just promise to do this for myself; I promised to do it for other women too. I wanted to share what I was learning and help them understand that taking care of yourself and becoming an active manager of the body that God has given you isn't selfish—it's essential. And that is what this book is about.

Back when I made that vow, the "other women" I was thinking about were the other soccer moms and my close friends and family members. But today, God has led me on a path in my life and blessed me with the opportunity to share this important message with women everywhere. You may think, *Why are you any different from any other fifty-five-year-old woman?* The only difference is that thanks to my husband's worldwide television show, *Dr. Phil*, I have the privilege of being able to talk to women all over the world about the issues I feel passionate about. I've had a chance to reach out in many ways—like speaking at the Women of Faith conference and appearing on shows like *Rachael Ray*—and the more women I talk to, the more I'm inspired to *keep* talking. My feeling is that because God has given me this unique opportunity, it would be selfish for me not to seize it. Even if just one thing in this book changes the life of just one woman, it is my obligation to share what I've learned. I feel very strongly about that.

In these pages, I'm going to tell you the most important things that have influenced my physical, mental, emotional, and spiritual journey through this life. We are certainly going to talk about some fun things in these pages, such as hair, makeup, and fashion, but it's important to build all of these outward manifestations on a solid foundation of good health and well-being. One reason I'm passionate about this is because I know that in order to be the best wife, mother, daughter, sister, employee, or anything else you want to be, you have to first take care of yourself. Phillip has always said that we are like bank accounts—if all we ever do is make withdrawals of time, emotion, and energy for everyone else and we never put anything back, we will end up emotionally bankrupt. By taking care of your health, you give an amazing gift to those who love and care about you. That's why I say to you that if you love your children—and I know you do—take care of their mother first. If you love your husband, take care of his wife first. If you love your parents, take care of their daughter first.

In the seven seasons of the *Dr. Phil* show, I've had the pleasure of taking many deserving women through makeovers. These transformations have varied from on-the-spot makeovers where we redo women's hair, makeup, or clothes to month-long (or longer) makeovers where we give the women access to top experts in areas such as fitness, nutrition, skin care, fashion, beauty, and health.

Though the whole process of working with these women is an honor for me (and a lot of fun too), it is what happens *after* the makeovers that I love the best. So many of the women call or write me when they return home and tell me that their makeovers were more than skin deep. Sure, they lost weight, got new haircuts, and discovered which clothes really flatter their figures. But so many of these women say their internal transformation was the most life changing. After many years of putting themselves last, they finally realize that they're worth some time, attention, and care. They have more confidence when they look and feel their best, and this improves every aspect of their lives. They tell me they finally feel like the women they were meant to be. One particular woman who had been part of a thirty-day makeover stands out in my mind. She came up to me after we taped the last show, held my hand, and with tears running down her cheeks said, "I will never, *ever* go back to the way I was. I am going to go forward with the new me. Thank you for changing my life."

What amazes me is that I always go into our makeover projects wanting to make a difference in these women's lives, but in the end these women make a difference in mine. They have inspired me to continue sharing this message of self-care, not self-neglect, and they have inspired me to write this book. The other women who motivated me to put my pen to paper are the thousands and thousands who e-mail me every month. These are women who want to change their lives but aren't sure how.

There are certain sentiments I hear over and over again, and it breaks my heart that I can't personally help each one. Here are just a few examples of what these women are saying:

- "I'm forty-two years old, but feel like I'm sixty-two."
- "For years I've let myself go, and now I don't know how to get the old me back."
- "I have lost my glow."
- "I miss the woman I used to be."
- "I'm so afraid of getting older."
- "I want to feel healthy and alive again."
- "I feel like I am falling apart."
- "I want to have some sense of pride when I look in the mirror."
- "I want to make myself feel better so I can be the wife and mother my husband and children deserve."
- "When I look in the mirror I see three words: *tired, sad,* and *old.*"
- "I hate how I look so much that I hide in the house, too embarrassed to show myself to the world."

If you have any of these thoughts, you are not alone. After reading many, many e-mails like these, I knew I had to write a book not only to answer the questions women have about what I personally do, but also to share some of the important resources I have found and to remind you that you are worth it. It's time to take yourself off life's back burner! My mother's early death taught me that it doesn't make you a better wife or parent if you're sacrificing everything—including your health, soul, and spirit—for your family. I want you to join me and get excited about living your life in a passionate, happy, and healthy way.

This is a book for women of all ages, because I believe it's never too early to become an active manager of your health and well-being. And I feel like I'm proof of that. Today, as a fifty-five-year-old woman, I thank my much younger self because what I did in my twenties, thirties, and forties has really paid off. In my twenties, my motivation for exercising and eating right may have been more about looking good in my hip huggers, but still I'm thankful that I laid the foundation for those healthy habits. And now, my reasons go well beyond how my clothes fit. When my mother passed away in my thirties, my focus shifted to my health. But I also looked ahead. I realized that I didn't want to spend years raising my kids and caring for my family and then, after they were grown, look in the mirror to see a woman I could barely recognize, a woman who looked old and felt useless. Instead, I've set my life in a way that I look forward to the future. That said, I wholeheartedly believe that it's never too late to start taking care of yourself by taking control of your health and well-being. Every day is a new chance to live your healthiest, happiest life, and I know that what I continue to do today will pay off in my sixties and seventies. I'm always paying attention to my body, learning new things, and changing how I care for myself accordingly.

I also believe in being proactive in my health care. If I don't feel well, I don't sit around worrying about what's wrong with me. I take action. And even when I feel fine, I manage my health like my life depends on it. After all, I realized, if I'm not going to do it, no one else is. So every year, I get a complete physical, Pap smear, and mammogram, and twice a year I visit the dentist. I have blood work done to check my cholesterol levels and blood enzymes, and I have my hormone levels checked every three months (but more on that in chapter 5). I've had a bone density scan, which checks for signs of osteoporosis; a colonoscopy, which looks for colon cancer; and a heart scan, which checks for blocked arteries. I've even had a full-body scan—a noninvasive, painless procedure in which a machine scans your body to see if anything is growing where it shouldn't be. Even if you don't have the best health care coverage, you can still be proactive by getting checkups from doctors or clinics on your plan or seeking out low cost or free screenings and seminars at local hospitals, clinics, community centers, or health centers. For example, you can find free skin cancer screenings through the American Academy of Dermatology or free or low cost mammograms through the National Breast and Cervical Cancer Early Screening Program.

I'm also conscious of my family's medical history, since so many diseases are genetic. My mother died of heart disease, my father died of cancer, and my twin brother had a triple bypass just six years ago. Family history is a risk factor for all of these things, but I can't control genetics. So I choose to focus on the risk factors I *can* control by doing things like eating right, exercising, taking vitamins, managing my hormones, and not smoking or drinking alcohol. I also do monthly self breast exams and skin exams. Phillip calls me the "research queen" because I also keep up on the latest health information by reading books, visiting my favorite Web sites, and talking to many of the doctors, pharmacists, and alternative medicine experts I know. Naturally, I don't think that I can control *everything*, but I believe in doing my best.

Now, let me be clear. I am not saying I'm perfect by any means. I love chocolate and a glass of champagne as much as the next girl, and I eat bread every day (yes, every day). I'm sure if I had a really clean diet, I'd be ten pounds lighter, but giving up the foods I love is just not worth it to me. My goal is not to be perfect (whatever that is) but to have realistic expectations about how to achieve my healthiest and happiest life. I'm also not saying that taking care of yourself can change you completely. We inherit our mother's thighs or our grandma's hips, and there's often only so much you can do to change that. As a result, let's not waste time beating ourselves up; instead, I say love those hips and move on.

This goes along with my belief that you choose how you live your life and how you approach it. Every day is a choice. You can wake up feeling negative and afraid of the future, or you can wake up and say, "Today, I choose to do everything I can to have peace, love, and joy in my life." Choice is a *big* part of my life. I know that God has a plan for me, and I choose to be happy and excited about that plan. I don't take it for granted that he has given me another day. Instead, I choose to take care of myself and know that it's not selfish to put myself first. You can do that too. It's okay to take a break from your fast-paced life and not answer the phone every time it rings or respond instantly to every e-mail that you receive. It's okay to take a little time for yourself and tell the kids, "No, I'm not driving you to your friend's house right now" or to let the laundry go for a day. You don't have to always have perfect groceries in your refrigerator, and your kids don't have to love every meal you serve. Though I know that I was put on this earth to be a wife and mother, and though raising my two sons was a job I took seriously, there were times when I did let the laundry go or ordered take-out so I could recharge my batteries and do what I needed to care for myself. Now as young men of twenty-nine and twenty-two years old, my sons Jay and Jordan are none the worse for it.

That said, sometimes we don't even realize that we need a break or some "me time." Women are so used to running, running, running, and living with sky-high stress levels that we come to believe that it's normal to feel worn out, exhausted, and anxious. I have even heard women say that they're "supposed" to feel sluggish, tired, stressed, and fat, among other things, and they rationalize it by saying, "I'm busy" or "I'm a mom." But you don't have to feel that way. In my opinion, you're not supposed to feel exhausted and worn out; you're supposed to feel empowered and in control. Yes, you are busy; yes, you have a job; and yes, you are a daughter, wife, and mother. But being all those things is all the more reason you need to feel your best and be your healthiest. You need all your strength to juggle the demands of your life, so getting yourself in the best shape possible will help. After all, if you're not taking care of yourself, then everyone else in your life is not receiving the best of you. I want to help you change all that.

In this book, we're going to talk about various topics including fitness, nutrition, skin care, hormones, makeup, hair, and fashion. Of course, you may not need to work on all these areas of your life. But if you do, it can be too overwhelming to tackle too many at once. Instead, focus on the one or two areas that are of biggest concern to you or that you're the most motivated to improve. Once you see how great you feel by making some changes in one aspect of your life, it's like a snowball effect, and you'll actually want to make changes in the others. As I said earlier, my goal is not to tell you what to do, but to share with you what I've done and what works for me. This includes expert advice and information on products and treatments (though I have no financial or commercial interest in any of the products, services, or professionals mentioned in this book). Then I hope to inspire you to figure out what works for *you*.

I am not an expert in these subjects, but I am an expert in how these things relate to me. I want you to become an expert in you. In order to help you do just that, I've assembled a panel of experts who will share their advice throughout the pages of this book. But these aren't just any experts, and I didn't choose to include them only because they had good credentials and fabulous résumés (though they do). These are the people I have personally consulted to help me feel and look my best. I am grateful to have them in my life, and I am grateful that they agreed to share their insight and wisdom with you.

So let me introduce you to your panel of experts:

Robert Reames, CSCS, D, CN, RTS1, CPT, is a personal trainer and nutritionist who is also the official trainer and nutritionist for the Dr. Phil Ultimate Weight Loss Challenge, as well as the author of *Make Over Your Metabolism* and creator of the Robert Reames Lifestyle Transformation System DVD series. I met Robert just two days after we moved from Dallas to Los Angeles. As you'll see throughout the book, I like to be focused and organized, so just a week before we moved, I called a gym equipment store to arrange for them to come to my house the day we arrived to put together the home gym equipment I was bringing from Dallas. When the man came to assemble it, I asked him if he knew any personal trainers and he recommended Robert. He came to my house the very next day, and we've been working out together ever since.

Janet Harris is a renowned aesthetician and the owner of the Skin Rejuvenation Center in Beverly Hills as well as the creator of an array of unique skin-care products. Her expertise in all things skin never ceases to amaze me. Prior to owning her own spa, Janet worked in the offices of several plastic surgeons helping patients heal post-op; and it was there that she learned so much about how the skin works, heals, and rejuvenates, as well as what not to do to your complexion. What I love about Janet, and why I connected with her immediately, is that she does not jump on the bandwagon of the latest product or treatment. She doesn't care about hyping the latest anti-aging trend, but instead is thoughtful and methodical in the treatments she offers and the advice she dispenses.

Jim Hrncir, RPh, is much more than a pharmacist. When I first met him, he was a friend of the family who happened to own the Las Colinas Pharmacy Compounding and Wellness Center in Irving, Texas. I'd heard people talk about how brilliant he was and describe him as one of the pioneers in pharmaceutical and nutritional compounding. But it wasn't until I was going through menopause (which you'll read a lot more about in chapter 5) and needed his expertise that I saw it for myself. His advice put me on the right path to good health, and for that I am grateful. Even though he's in Texas and I'm in California, we're always in touch. It amazes me that more than ten years later, I still learn something from him every time we talk.

Prudence Hall, MD, is the Founder and Medical Director of The Hall Center In Santa Monica, California, specializing in gynecology and functional medicine. The Hall Center is a place I credit for helping me feel fabulous at the ripe, young age of fifty-five. From my first meeting with Dr. Hall, I knew I was in the presence of a doctor who respects her patients and treats them as individuals. Her extensive knowledge in integrated healing and functional medicine has not only put her on the frontier of modern advances for menopause and rejuvenation therapies, but has helped me manage my hormones naturally, something that is very important to me.

Howard Liebowitz, MD, is Medical Director of The Hall Center in Santa Monica, California specializing in Functional Medicine, Anti-Aging Medicine and Alternative Internal Medicine. For more than twenty years, he worked as an emergency and trauma physician and was the medical director at The Centinela Hospital Fitness Institute, testing professional athletes.

Today, his focus is managing health through nutrition and achieving optimal health as well as slowing the aging process. Like Dr. Hall, he cares deeply and sincerely for his patients, and that was obvious to me the first time we met. Because of what he has taught me about nutrition, hormones, and so much more, I am living my healthiest and happiest life today.

Frank Lawlis, PhD, is a psychologist, researcher, and sleep expert who is the author of several books, including *The Stress Answer* and *The IQ Answer*. I met Frank back in 1975 when he was one of Phillip's professors in graduate school. They had a unique bond back then and have maintained a very close relationship through the years. This has allowed me to get to know Frank and to benefit from his insight and wisdom. Today, he is the head of the advisory board of the *Dr. Phil* show, and his expertise has made a difference in the lives of so many guests on the show, as well as my own.

Matthew Vanleeuwen is a Hollywood makeup artist whose celebrity clients include Heidi Klum, Scarlett Johansson, Salma Hayek, Kate Beckinsale, and Mariska Hargitay. His expert hand transforms the faces of top celebrities and models. As a result, his work has graced the covers of major magazines and appeared in top movies and television shows. Over the years, he has become a friend who has also done my makeup for very special occasions, such as my son Jay's wedding. What I love about Matthew is that his philosophy is not to approach the face by what needs to taken away or fixed, but to focus on its strengths. When he told me that he loves crow's-feet and sees them as a symbol of experience, I knew it was the start of a very lovely friendship.

Steven "Cojo" Cojocaru is a fashion guru and author of the *Red Carpet Diaries: Confessions of a Glamour Boy* and *Glamour, Interrupted: How I Became* *the Best Dressed Patient in Hollywood.* When a producer on the *Dr. Phil* show suggested I work with Cojo for one of our makeover stories, I happily agreed; and from the minute we met, we had a unique connection. Despite the fact that he works the red carpet for *Entertainment Tonight* and mingles with top designers and celebrities, Cojo never fails to give amazing fashion advice to real women. Yet more than his fashion sense, smarts, and sense of humor, I admire Cojo's ability to face adversity in his life—he has had two kidney transplants—and triumph.

Lucie Doughty is a celebrity colorist. I was looking for someone to color my hair, so I asked Matthew Vanleeuwen for recommendations. After all, he was always working on movie sets and photo shoots, so I figured he'd know someone fabulous. I was right. In all the years that I've been coloring and highlighting my hair (and as you'll see from chapter 6, it's been a long time), Lucie was the first colorist who was able to give me highlights that I really like. Because I have a lot of red in my hair, I'd usually wind up with gold or copper highlights when what I wanted was a soft blonde color. Lucie painted her first streak on my hair three years ago, and I haven't looked back since.

This group of experts has led me on a path to a healthier and happier life, and I hope their insight and my personal stories will inspire you to do the same. I firmly believe that your health is everything, and if you are living your healthiest life, you will live your happiest. Every moment of every day, God blesses us with another chance to get healthy. So let's take that first step, shall we?

2

What's Fitness
Got to Do with It?

It was the night before my wedding, and I was at my parents' house trying on my dress for one of my sisters. "I need to lose weight," I said, pinching a roll of fat on my upper thigh. "Just look at this!" I glanced over at my sister and was stunned to see that her eyes were filled with tears.

"Robin, lose it when it's five pounds, not fifty," she said with a sad and defeated expression—an expression I'll never forget. Despite the fact that my thighs carried a negligible amount of fat, I knew what she was trying to tell me. Just four years earlier, it had been her wedding day, and she had walked down the aisle looking radiant in her slim-fitting white gown. Yet she spent the ensuing years doing what so many wonderful women do: putting everyone else first and herself last. Now she was forty pounds overweight. The extra pounds not only weighed on her body, but also on her soul. They had changed her perky personality. Her words and expression were urging me to do things differently, and I vowed that I would. Even though I was thrilled to be marrying Phillip and excited about my new life as part of a couple, I also knew that I had to take care of myself. I had to do it for myself and, yes, I had to do it for my sister.

Though my mother's death eight years later really made me step up my efforts to stay healthy, that moment with my sister was pivotal. Between my mother and three older sisters, I grew up getting a good, hard look at my genetics and how I would probably age if I *didn't* take care of myself. All four of them struggled with their weight and neglected themselves both physically and emotionally. Even though I also take after my father, who was very lean and had dense muscle mass, it's no accident that I've always been trim. But with genetics against me, I could just as easily have been battling my weight all my life, especially after going through two pregnancies and then menopause. The reason I'm not putting on weight has nothing to do with luck and everything to do with a lot of sweat—literally—on my part. I'm always amazed when I hear women say that it's okay that they're fat because gaining weight is a fact of life. I don't believe that for a minute and think I'm proof of that.

I started exercising in my twenties and know that doing so has really paid off in my fifties. In fact, at the age of fifty-five, I'm at one of my healthiest and happiest times of my life. Admittedly, I don't have the muscles in my legs that I used to, my waist is a bit wider, and of course I could always stand to drop a little weight because the camera adds ten pounds. (I can't count how many people have told me that I look so much leaner in person!) But the important thing is that I feel like I have the best body for *me*. I'm strong and fit, and I sleep like a rock because of it. And I love the energy I have because I've taken care of myself. I'm certainly not obsessed with exercise. I don't work out on Sundays, when I travel, or on vacation, and there are days when I can't stand to lace up my tennis shoes. But for the most part, I've exercised consistently from the time I got married until now and have reaped the results. It's a lot like saving money. You stash a dollar here and a dollar there, and over the months and years all that investing pays off. The same is true for exercise.

Of course, working out is important for many reasons that go well beyond toned triceps and a flat stomach. I not only want to look good in my favorite jeans, but I also exercise regularly so that in five, ten, fifteen, or more years I can continue to be productive and active and do things I enjoy, like playing tennis, traveling, and chasing after my future grandchildren. If you feel the same way, then making exercise a regular part of your life is a must.

Many, many studies suggest that regular exercise can reduce your risk of diseases such as heart disease, cancer, diabetes, and osteoporosis; improve cholesterol, blood pressure, insomnia, and depression; and strengthen your immune system, among many other benefits. Exercise can also lift your mood because it produces feel-good brain chemicals called endorphins. It may not work for everyone, but I know that when I'm stressed or over-whelmed, there's nothing like a good sweat session to improve my mood, calm me down, or help me see things more clearly. (In fact, I've gotten some of my best ideas while power walking!)

This is one reason I've always encouraged Phillip to play tennis after work. I have friends who say, "I can't believe you let him play tennis so often." This isn't about "letting" him do anything. Besides the fact that I never tell Phillip what to do or not do (and vice versa), I know that playing tennis is the best way for him to de-stress and that he feels so much better when he's able to exercise. (And don't we all benefit when our husbands are calm and happy?) If all those reasons haven't convinced you to slip on your sweatpants, maybe this one will: because exercise increases circulation

WHAT'S AGE GOT TO DO WITH IT?

throughout the body, it can give your skin a youthful glow and improve your complexion.

Robin's Way

Phillip has burned quite a few CDs for me, and then I transfer some of them to my iPod. My three favorite artists are Tina Turner, Cher, and Celine Dion, so I always have their songs on my iPod—especially the high-energy oldies. I also have all the victory songs from *American Idol* and always put a few songs from movie soundtracks like *Dreamgirls*.

Now, I know plenty of women who say that they feel selfish taking time away from their families, jobs, and other responsibilities to exercise. But, as you'll hear me say often in this book, it is not selfish to take care of yourself. If you're going for a walk so your heart is healthier and you will be alive longer to take care of your loved ones, that's not selfish. If you're exercising so you feel lean and strong and thus more confident, that's not selfish. A happier more confident mom, wife, or friend is going to be a better one. And if you're exercising to become stronger so that you can kick a ball, ride a bike, and keep up with your kids, well, I don't think anyone would call that selfish.

Sometimes women tell me that exercise is too expensive or that they think the reason I'm in good shape is because I live in Hollywood and have access to personal trainers and gyms. All that may be true *today*, but it's only been the case for the last six years since I moved to California. I've been exercising long before I could even afford a good pair of tennis shoes or sports bra! When Phillip and I were first married, we had no money and lived in an apartment that was about five hundred square feet. But at night I'd hook my feet under the legs of a little metal kitchen chair and do sit-ups. Other days I'd sweat along with Jane Fonda's workout videos that I borrowed from the library. Years later, when our son Jay was a baby, we still didn't have much money or space. Yet I exercised by stepping up on a wooden stool one hundred times in a row. That didn't cost me a thing, and though it may not have been fancy, it was some aerobic workout (and elicited lots of giggles from Jay!).

I'm positive that those small efforts in my twenties helped lay a foundation for the healthy life I live today. In fact, your twenties is an ideal time to instill those good habits, and the sooner you start working out the better. A lot of research suggests this, but I was intrigued by a recent study of sixty-five thousand women from Washington University in St. Louis. Researchers there found that girls and women who worked out regularly between the ages of twelve and thirty-five had a 23 percent lower risk of premenopausal breast cancer than women of the same age who didn't exercise.[1] Plus, with youth on your side, your body is still flexible enough to try new and different activities and your mind is more open to doing so. That's key because experimenting is the best way to find something you like to do. And, trust me, liking what you do is the difference between sticking with exercise and making a million excuses not to.

Having that adventurous twentysomething mind-set is how I discovered tennis when I was twenty-six years old. I remember it like it was yesterday. Phillip came home from work, and there I was holding Jay in one hand and vacuuming with the other. (That's how I did everything back then: cradling Jay in one arm and doing something else with the other.) "I know if it were up to you, you'd hold that baby all the time," Phillip said. "But you need to get out and do something for *you*." He was right. I loved being a mother and wife and could have devoted every minute of every day to that, but I also knew that in addition to those roles, I was still a woman. And if you're a woman, you need to take care of yourself.

I'd always wanted to take up tennis (Phillip had been an avid player for eight years) and thought it would be a fun way to stay in shape. But since lessons from a pro at a private club were too pricey for our budget, I called Midwestern State University, a college in our area, and asked the physical education department if someone from their tennis team was available to teach me. From my first day on the court, I was hooked and started playing tennis two times a week. The lessons were only about ten dollars an hour, and I'd have Phillip, my parents, or my in-laws watch Jay. To get more time on the court and feed my competitive side, I entered tournaments in the beginners' bracket and joined a local women's league. Besides the fabulous workout I got, I loved that time to myself and felt such a sense of confidence and achievement because I learned something new. I even made some good friends—friends who were my opponents. The story of my first tournament is a perfect example of the difference between men and women, but also an example of what I love about exercising with other people.

I was playing singles against another woman, and we each won a set (I took the first, she the second). By the third set, which I lost, Phillip had finished his own match at an adjacent court and had come to watch.

"What happened?" he asked.

"Well, I won the first set, and the second set was really close," I explained. "Before the third, we were both exhausted and hungry, so we took a break. I shared my water and my protein bar with her, and then we got back on the court."

"You *shared* your food and water with her?" Phillip asked.

"Yes. Can you believe that poor thing forgot to bring herself some water and food?" I told him. "We were both exhausted, so it was a good thing I had enough."

"Robin, you don't break bread with the opponent!" Phillip said.

"What?"

"Your opponent was starving and had no energy, and you fed her and gave her water, which is why she came back and beat you."

"Oh, that's okay," I said. "She was so sweet and she's a mom, too, so we had lots to talk about and had a great time." Now I am a competitive person so I wanted to win, but the exercise and social aspect of playing tennis were also important to me. Each week, I looked forward not only to my lesson, but also to seeing the women from my league and having some girl talk. Today, there are so many ways to find other people to exercise with. You can try local or church leagues (I joined a softball team for a short time), group exercise classes at a local community center or gym, or a walking or running club.

I have talked to many women in their twenties and early thirties who say they don't need to exercise because they're blessed with superfast metabolisms. To the envy of their friends, they can eat pretty much whatever they want and not gain an ounce. However, after the age of thirty our metabolisms slow down by an estimated 2 percent per decade,[2] so just because yours is good when you're young doesn't mean it will be like that forever.

I hate to be the bearer of such bad news, but I know this firsthand. For most of my life, I was so skinny that I couldn't gain weight no matter how much I ate. In fact, I remember wishing that I'd weigh over one hundred pounds by my high school graduation! But by my midthirties, my metabolism slowed down a bit and I gained weight more easily. Still, I don't think my metabolism changed as much as it could have, and I credit that to the research I did in my early twenties. With the genetic crystal ball I had (my mother and three older sisters), I researched how I could keep my metabolism happily humming along and learned that three things were important: cardiovascular exercise, strength training, and avoiding yo-yo diets at all costs. The latter is critical and as a result, I've never been on a diet in my life. (We'll chat more about food and nutrition in chapter 3).

When it came to cardio exercise, I couldn't get enough. After all, my mother died of a heart attack, so keeping my heart healthy was a top priority. I really liked power walking, aerobics classes, and cardio machines at the local YMCA. I also loved doing a combination of running for one minute and walking for four minutes on the treadmill that we eventually bought for our home. We didn't have much room, so I put it in the bathroom that connected Jay's room and Jordan's nursery. I situated the treadmill so it was facing the mirror and put a little television in the bathroom too. Jay was seven years old at the time and Jordan was a newborn, so my hands were full all day long. By evening I was ready for a little time to myself, so I'd fix dinner, the four of us would eat together, and then about an hour later I'd hand the boys over to Phillip and get on my treadmill for forty-five minutes to an hour. If Phillip was traveling or working late, my mother-in-law would come over and babysit. That time to myself was sacred, and I worked hard to keep it that way.

Years later, I joined a gym so I could use a variety of cardio machines. When I was about thirty-six years old, I noticed that I was gaining a few pounds. Normally when that happened, I'd cut back at dinner for a few days and the pounds would drop off. But to my chagrin that technique didn't work in my midthirties, so I decided to do even more cardio than usual. Every day I'd go to the gym, get on the stair climber, and huff and puff on that machine for more than an hour. I didn't notice any changes in my body, but I kept going. After two weeks of this, one of the gym's personal trainers approached me.

"Do you mind if I ask you something?" she said.

"Of course not."

"What exactly is your goal with these workouts?"

"I want to lose a few pounds," I explained, huffing and puffing and barely able to get the words out.

"I thought so," she said, nodding her head. Then she enlightened me: she said I was actually working *too hard* to lose weight. Can you imagine that? She explained to me that there is something called an "optimum workout zone," which is when you're exercising at an intensity of between 65 percent and 85 percent of your maximum heart rate. When you're in that zone, you typically burn more overall calories and fat and, as a result, lose weight. The most accurate way to make sure you're in this zone (which is different for each person) is with a heart-rate monitor. But even without one, the trainer said she knew I was overtraining because I was so breathless I could hardly carry on a conversation with her. When you're in the right zone, you should be slightly breathless but still able to talk. My intense workouts were perfect if I were training for a marathon, she told me, but they were not going to get me into my skinny jeans anytime soon. On a scale of 1 to 10 with 10 being the point of total exhaustion and 1 being no effort at all, I think I was an 11 or 12.

That same day, I went out and bought myself a heart-rate monitor, and from then on I scaled back the intensity of my workouts and stayed in my optimum workout zone, which is between 136 and 152. (See pages 40–41 in "Answers from the Expert" for the formula that will help you figure out *your* optimum workout zone.) I also liked to do sprint workouts—and still do—so sometimes I'd stay in my optimum zone for four minutes and then spend one minute in the 170–180 range. Because you're only there for a very brief period, it actually helps boost metabolism and fat burning without overtraining. Wouldn't you know it, in less than a week those stubborn pounds started coming off!

I told that story to Robert Reames, who has been my personal trainer and Phillip's for the last six and half years and is the official trainer and nutritionist for the Dr. Phil Ultimate Weight Loss Challenge. He's also written a book about metabolism, *Make Over Your Metabolism*,[3] so he nodded in agreement and said that being too focused on cardio is a common fitness mistake made by women in their twenties and early thirties. Cardio is great for you—it works your heart and helps burn fat. But there's another element that's crucial for women of all ages, and that's strength training. This means you provide some form of resistance for your muscles, and there are several ways to do it. The least expensive way is to use your own body weight by doing good old calisthenics like pushups, squats, lunges, and pull-ups (think middle school gym class). The other option is to use free weights or dumbbells (you can even use soup cans or full water bottles), and the third is to use weight machines, typically found at the gym.

Robin's Rx At the end of an exercise class I used to take, the teacher would say, "Take a few seconds to thank your body for its hard work." I found that so powerful, because no matter how critical I was of myself at that moment (because I saw a little roll hanging over my pants or struggled with an exercise), it brought me to a state of gratitude and appreciation for my efforts. That class was a long time ago, but to this day I take a few minutes after my workouts to close my eyes and thank my body for its hard work. I focus on how my body has not only carried me through a tough workout, but also carried and created two beautiful children. Lastly, I thank God for blessing me with good health and strength.

Many women worry that strength training will bulk them up, but ask the experts and you'll realize that's pretty rare. Men have lots of testosterone floating around their bodies, which is what gives them those big, ropey muscles, but the majority of women don't have enough of this hormone to even get close. Instead, strength training tones and firms your body and, just as important, makes your life easier because you're strong enough to carry your groceries, lift your children, take out the trash, or move your couch. It also builds bone density, which can help ward off osteoporosis later in life.

I started strength training in my early thirties on the weight machines at my local YMCA and loved the tone and definition my muscles had. I also appreciated how this muscle would keep my metabolism in top shape.

Robert has a great way of explaining how this works, and he does so by talking about acute and chronic calorie burning. "Acute calorie burning" refers to the calories your body is torching both *while* you're doing some form of aerobic exercise and for about two to three hours after your workout. (Yes, you're still burning calories even when you stop!) But when you build muscle, you experience something called "chronic calorie burning." Because it takes more energy to develop and maintain muscle than it does to maintain fat, you're actually burning calories all the time whether you're watching TV, at your desk, or even sleeping. In fact, for every pound of muscle you gain, you burn up to forty to fifty more calories per day, a metabolism boost that's especially important after your thirtieth birthday when women tend to naturally lose 1 percent of muscle mass per year. By strength training, you maintain this muscle and then some!

Pregnancy is another reason women gain weight in their twenties and thirties and keep it on well beyond their baby's first birthday. In fact, research shows that even nine years after giving birth, the average woman weighs about fourteen pounds more than she did before she got pregnant. I was pregnant with Jay when I was twenty-six years old and with Jordan when I was thirty-three. Each pregnancy was totally different mostly because I was health conscious and exercised during one and wasn't during the other.

Prior to getting pregnant with Jay, I'd been working full-time and going to school at night and knew I'd need a break before entering the wonderful world of motherhood. So when I found out I was pregnant, and Phillip and I figured we could get by financially if I quit my job, I did just that with the goal of simply enjoying my nine months as a mom-to-be. And, boy, did I enjoy it! Once I got over the first trimester of horrible morning sickness, my normally big appetite was even bigger, and I gave in to every craving. I ate candy (my favorites were Sweet Tarts and red licorice), cheeseburgers, chicken fried steak, and unusual combinations like pancakes smothered in peanut butter. I remember one night when Phillip and I went out to dinner and I ordered two entrées while he just had one. (But being the smart husband of a very hormonal pregnant woman, he didn't say a peep!) Then a huge tornado hit our town, and a couple we were close friends with lost their home. They moved in with us, and since the wife was also pregnant, the two of us spent lots of time sitting around at home and eating. As you can imagine, this nine-month eating spree resulted in a weight gain of almost eighty pounds (yes, you read that correctly). That's a lot of weight for any woman, but it seems like even more when you're just 5 foot 3 inches. I felt sluggish and exhausted all the time, and in the last month, my feet got so big that none of my shoes fit and I had to borrow my sister-in-law's flip-flops.

My second pregnancy was quite a contrast to the first. By then, I had a seven-year-old to keep up with and had become an avid exerciser, so my focus was on being as healthy as possible. After dropping Jay at school, I played tennis three mornings a week (until my fourth month) and did a lot of power walking around my neighborhood well into my seventh or eighth month. Phillip and I would get in the car and map out a one-to-two-mile-long route (though today you can easily go online and do this). As a result, I gained only thirty-three pounds (which is in line with the twenty-five to thirty-five-pound range doctors suggest for a normal-sized woman). Today, experts recommend exercising while pregnant because it may reduce fatigue and morning sickness, provide much-needed energy, lift your mood, make labor and delivery easier, and help you shed that baby weight more quickly once your bundle of joy arrives. I reaped all those benefits with my second pregnancy and felt fabulous. I had energy to burn!

Robin's Rx If you are time crunched and can't get your workouts in consistently, studies have shown that breaking up the recommended thirty minutes of physical activity per day into three ten-minute increments throughout your day will give you the same and or better results than doing the thirty minutes all at once. Why? Because you can achieve a higher intensity level in each of the shorter ten-minute time blocks and you're giving yourself that metabolic boost of physical activity at different points throughout the day.

From the time Jay and Jordan were little, I stressed the importance of fitness. I did so believing that if you make exercise a family priority early on, your kids will view it as a normal part of life and will be more likely to exercise themselves. This was important to me since obesity runs in Phillip's family, and my mom died of a heart attack. As a result, both of my boys played sports all through school—everything from basketball to baseball to lacrosse—and today as young men in their twenties, Jordan works out about five times a week (and has the healthiest diet of any twenty-two-year-old I know), and Jay plays tennis and golf.

Though I kept exercising in my forties, several of my walking and tennis buddies cut back or gave up altogether. By then, they were caring for their kids *and* their own parents as well as juggling marriages, careers, and social lives. Many of them were amazed that I kept exercising because they said they just didn't have the energy. I was just as busy, but for me, exercise was and always has been a good source of the energy I need to power through my hectic daily life. What's so interesting, according to a new study from the University of Georgia, is that low-intensity exercise may be all you need to feel more alert. In the study participants did just twenty minutes of this type of exercise and found that their fatigue decreased by 65 percent while their energy levels got a 20 percent boost! Back then, my workout of choice was walking. Every morning after I got the kids off to school, I walked the neighborhood alone or with friends. Other mornings, I played tennis.

Then when I was forty-eight and Phillip got offered his own show, we moved our family from Texas to Beverly Hills. All of a sudden I was busy going to tapings of the show (I have never missed one) and driving Jordan, who was fifteen years old, to and from school and after-school activities. Suddenly, midmorning walks didn't fit my schedule. This happens to women all the time. Our lives change, and though it can be daunting, we need to take a second look at our priorities and make a few tweaks. It would have been easy to skip my workout altogether, but I knew how much I needed it for my physical and mental health. Though it was tough at first, I decided to get up at 5:00 a.m.—an hour earlier than I used to— and walk on my treadmill. There were many mornings when I really had to push myself out of my warm, cozy bed, but I knew that if I could just get through those first fifteen minutes I'd be okay. I'm not sure why, but something happens to me after hitting that sixteen-minute mark where I go from trudging along to feeling like I can stay on that treadmill for hours. So I'd do a warm-up and then intervals of walking for four minutes and running for one (which is called interval training). For me, running for an hour was just not something I could or wanted to do. But simply running for one or two minutes every four minutes seemed easier and put less impact on my joints. I'd tell myself, "You can do anything for one minute" and then I'd be done and get a little reprieve as I walked for four minutes. This up and down really elevates your heart rate and burns more calories than you would just exercising at one steady pace.

I also prevent boredom—of my mind *and* body—by including variety in my workouts, which is why I took up Pilates at the age of fifty. Created in the early twentieth century by the dancer Joseph Pilates, this method of exercise focuses on the core muscles, alignment of the spine, and deep breathing. It really teaches you to use both your breath and your mind to make changes in your body, and it hits every muscle from head to toe. I saw my stomach flatten, my arms tone up, and my sagging butt lift. (It may not be as high as it used to be, but I'll take it.) My posture also improved greatly.

Robin's Rx Bad posture makes you look older and heavier, while good posture can make you look at least five pounds slimmer. This Pilates move can help you stand taller: place your arms behind your back, clasp your hands together, and pull down so that your shoulders go back and down. Not only have I benefited from this, but so has Phillip. One day during a taping of the show, I watched him walk across the stage and realized that his posture was slightly hunched over and making him look older than his years. The next day, I encouraged him to take Pilates with me; and just a few months later, when I watched him walk on to the stage during the *Tonight Show*, he looked about ten years younger and ten pounds lighter.

Throughout my fitness journey, I've never been afraid to try new things and challenge myself, and I think that's the key to warding off boredom and staying fit. It's definitely what's kept me going all this time. As a result, I recently traded cardio sessions on the treadmill for heart-pumping kickboxing. I took it up at the suggestion of my trainer and was surprised at how much I loved that first class and how, after just three weeks of kicking and punching (and intense sweating), I've seen big changes. And though I haven't played tennis in ten years, I've dusted off my racket and am getting back to it. My point is that it's not so much what you do to get exercise; it's just doing something. It's making fitness a part of your life either through formal exercise or lifestyle changes like taking the stairs instead of the elevator, parking the car farther away from the store, and biking or walking to do errands rather than driving.

I plan to keep working out well into my golden years. If you're picking up this book at the age of fifty, sixty, seventy, or beyond, I want you to know that you *can* start working out now, even if you've never done it before. And it's not just me saying that; research actually backs it up. One interesting study came from Weill Cornell Medical Center in New York, where they found that adults who didn't start eating well and exercising until they were sixty-five or older still reduced their risk of heart disease, cancer, and osteoporosis.[4] And another survey of fifteen thousand women between the ages of 20 and 69 done by the University of Wisconsin found that those who exercised for at least six hours per week reduced their risk of invasive breast cancer by 23 percent (these were women without a family history of the disease).[5] What I find interesting is that researchers saw this protective effect whether the women exercised early in life or after menopause. As a result, their take-home message was, "It's never too late to exercise." Amen! After all, if you're in your sixties or seventies, this may be the first time in your life when you've been able to focus on yourself. Though I certainly think you should start taking care of yourself as soon as possible, I also think that no matter how old you are, today is the first day of the rest of your life; so why not start on a healthy foot?

I know it's easier said than done to tell you to fit fitness into your life, but here are some of the top tips that have helped me make it a priority over the years.

Schedule your workouts. Life tends to get busy, and if you don't make time for exercise, no one else is going to make it for you. Plus, as my trainer Robert says, "Life happens." On Sundays, I review my schedule for the upcoming week and put into my BlackBerry the days and times I plan to work out. This makes it a nonnegotiable event like a meeting or show taping, and if it's in there I'm less likely to schedule something at the same time or skip it.

Robin's Way

Following is an example of my typical weekly workout schedule. However, it varies depending on a change in my schedule or mood. (If I start to get bored of one form of exercise, I have no problem trying something new.)

- *Monday, Thursday, and Friday:* Pilates sessions and cardio on the Precor machine or treadmill.
- *Tuesday and Wednesday:* These are the days we tape the show, so I don't work out. But if it's a week when we're not taping, I may take a tennis lesson—California weather makes it nice to be outside.
- *Saturday:* Total body workout with Robert Reames. (See sample workout following.)
- *Sunday:* Rest

Buddy up. Often, working out with another person improves the chances that you'll stick with it. You can have one workout buddy, like a friend you meet every morning for a walk or a coworker who joins you at the gym during lunch, or you can find a group of like-minded women to help you break a sweat. I've always loved power walking with friends, and my daughter-in-law and I take tennis lessons and Pilates classes together. Even young kids can be fabulous fitness partners. I remember power walking with Jordan in a baby stroller. When the boys got older, they'd ride bikes while I walked. Of course, you can also kick a ball around your backyard or simply play a game of tag and get your heart racing (not to mention set a good example for and create lasting memories with your kids).

Consult with the experts. Not everyone has the money to spend on a personal trainer, but it is worth it to invest in even a few sessions with an expert who can show you proper form and exercises that will help you reach your goals. Even if you can't afford a trainer, talk to a friend or coworker who's an avid exerciser (or even that woman you admire at the gym). It's likely that the other person will be so flattered at being seen as an expert that he or she will be glad to offer advice to get you started.

Robin's Way

Here's a sample of the kind of total body workout I do with Robert:

- Five minute warm-up walking on the treadmill.
- Basic stretches for shoulders, back, and legs.
- Chest presses using 15-pound dumbbells and lying on an exercise ball. Three to four sets of 12–15 repetitions.
- Seated row on the exercise ball and using tubing for resistance. Three sets of 12–15 repetitions.
- Standing overhead dumbbell presses using 8–10 pound dumbbells. Three sets of 12–15 repetitions.
- Triceps dips off a bench. Two to three sets of 15 repetitions.
- Standing arm curls with 8–10-pound dumbbells. Three sets of 12–15.

- Four to five 30-second sprints on the treadmill at a pace of at least 6.5 miles per hour.
- Basic squats holding 8–10 pound dumbbells. Three sets of 15 repetitions.
- Lunges holding 8–10 pound dumbbells. Three sets of 15 repetitions on each leg.
- Abdominal crunches while lying on the ball. One to two sets of 20 repetitions.
- Abdominal crunches with side-to-side rotation while lying on the ball. One to two sets of 20 repetitions.
- Floor bicycles while lying on an exercise mat. One to two sets of 24 repetitions.
- Supermans while lying on an exercise mat. Two to three sets of 10-second static holds (this means holding the position where the arms and legs are as high off the ground as possible).
- Cool down with 3–5 minutes of stretches for shoulders, back, and legs, holding each stretch about 15–20 seconds.

Take notes. As a super organized woman, I love making lists and keeping notes, and the area of fitness is no exception. Not only do I plan out the week and write down when I'm going to exercise, but I keep track of each workout, what I did, and how I felt. I do this more for fun rather than as something rigid, but it does help when I have one of those days where I just don't feel like exercising. I look back over my notes and am reminded of how great a workout makes me feel. This written record also helps if I notice my pants are getting a little snug, because I can look back and see what's going on (say, four days of missed workouts or a week without cardio) and what I was doing at times when I was in better shape.

Tell others about your new fitness regimen. Sharing your plans to get fit helps you stay accountable. After all, if you're telling your husband, the women in your tennis group, coworkers, or even the checkout gal at the grocery store about your get-fit plan, they're going to keep you honest. On bridge day, you're less likely to skip your daily run because you know the ladies will inquire about it or you'll get out of bed for that morning workout because your husband will know if you didn't. For me, I am much more successful if I'm accountable to something, so when I was trying to shed the eighty pounds I gained while pregnant with Jay, I decided to bet Phillip one hundred dollars that I'd lose the weight by Christmas (which was just three and a half months later). Phillip worried that I'd be disappointed if I didn't lose it that quickly, but I knew saying it out loud to him was just the motivation I needed. And it worked. One week before Christmas I weighed in at a pound *less* than I did before I got pregnant.

Set a goal. Having a goal in mind is motivating because it gives you something to strive for. The specific goal can be anything from losing five pounds, running a 5K race, or just improving your fitness level. My Christmas goal was just the push I needed. Before that, the baby would cry in the middle of the night, and as I warmed his bottle, I'd heat myself a box of Mrs. Good Cookies. Setting my sights on a holiday in the not-too-distant future really helped me kick that cookie habit. In addition to long-term goals, it's important to set smaller ones. There are times when I do this by the week or by the day and tell myself, "This week I want to strength train three times" or "Today I want to run two minutes longer than yesterday."

Answers from the Expert

Robert Reames, CSCS, D, CN, RTS1, CPT, personal trainer and nutritionist, official trainer and nutritionist for the Dr. Phil Ultimate Weight Loss Challenge, author of *Make Over Your Metabolism*, and creator of the Robert Reames Lifestyle Transformation System DVD series.

The thought of starting a fitness program is overwhelming. Where should I start?

People are always looking for the magic bullet to weight loss and fitness, and the only magic bullet that works is commitment. Make the decision right this minute to consistently include physical activity in your life. Promise yourself that no matter what comes up, you will exercise a minimum of three times a week and that you'll be more physically active in day-to-day life (such as taking stairs instead of the elevator or walking your shopping cart back to the store rather than leaving it in the parking lot).

Take an inventory of the fitness options you have available. For example, do you have a park nearby or a school with a track? Do you have a neighbor who walks each morning and with whom you could tag along? Do you have a VCR or DVD player so you could borrow exercise tapes from the library or video store? Do you have a gym membership you haven't used in a while?

Start small and accept that what you can do now is good enough and is your personal best for that day. You can always build upon it. For example, if you can only walk around the block once or run for five minutes, that's fine. Next time you can walk around the block twice or run for six or seven minutes. Acknowledge all progress, and be proud of your efforts.

I want to start exercising as soon as possible. What's a good beginner plan to try?

Starting right now while you feel motivated is a great idea. Here's a fifteen-minute workout that you can do almost anytime and anywhere. You may not be able to complete the whole circuit or do as many of each exercise as listed, but look at this as your goal to shoot for. Simply do as much as you can, and come back and try again tomorrow.

- One to two minutes: Warm up by marching in place. For half the time, pump your arms; for the other half, push and pull them overhead.
- Thirty seconds to one minute: Side reaches with heel lift. Reach up and over to the left side of your body with your right arm as you lift your right heel off the floor. Then reach up and over to the right side with your left arm and lift your left heel off the floor. Alternate for thirty seconds to one minute.
- Thirty seconds to one minute: Do jumping jacks. For a low-impact version, alternate keeping one foot on the floor as arms go up in the air.
- Do two sets of 10–15 wall push-ups. Stand about an arm's length away from the wall and place hands on the wall at shoulder height. Bend arms as you bring your upper body toward the wall. As you progress, try doing push-ups on the floor on your knees, working up to standard push-ups balancing on your hands and toes.
- Do two sets of 10–15 chair squats. Stand in front of a chair with feet shoulder-width apart and arms hanging by your sides. Squat down as if you're going to sit in the chair, making sure your knees are over your first and second toe but never in front of your feet. Bend only as far as you can go, but never go deeper than having knees at

90-degree angles. As you progress, hold dumbbells or a couple of bottles or jugs of water for resistance.

- Do two to three sets of 10 chair dips. Sit upright at the edge of a sturdy chair with hands on either side of your thighs and palms facing the chair. Scoot your behind off the edge of the chair with legs bent and ankles directly in line with your knees. Bend elbows until they form 90-degree angles (or as close as you can get to that), pause and then return to start without sitting on the chair. As you bend your elbows, keep your back as close to the chair as possible.

- Do two sets of 10 floor bridges. Lie on your back with legs bent and feet flat on the floor. Press your feet into the floor as you lift your hips toward the ceiling, pause and lower your body toward the floor. As you progress, do bridge with feet elevated on a chair or bench.

- Do three sets of 15 crunches. Lie on your back with knees bent and feet flat on the floor. Bend your arms and place your hands behind your head. Slowly lift your upper body so that your shoulder blades are off the floor, pause, and return to start without completely lying on the floor.

- Three to five minutes: March in place raising your knees and pumping your arms and standing up straight.

How can I measure my success?

You can do this by getting on the scale and/or taking measurements of your body. Some people like to have an item of clothing, like a favorite pair of pants or jeans, that they try on regularly to check for changes in their bodies. You can also give yourself a basic fitness test today to establish your baseline fitness level and then repeat it every month or two to see how much stronger you've gotten. Here's how:

- For one minute, see how many chair squats you can do. Stand in front of a chair with feet shoulder-width apart and arms by your sides. With most of your weight on your heels, squat down as if you're about to sit in the chair, but return to standing just as your butt grazes the chair (rather than actually sitting).
- For one minute, see how many push-ups you can do. If you can't do a standard push-up where you're balancing on your toes and hands and lowering your body until your chest hits the floor, then do wall push-ups where you stand about an arm's length from the wall with hands shoulder-width apart at shoulder height.
- Walk or run one mile as fast as you can.
- Test your balance by standing on one leg and timing yourself. Switch legs and repeat. Work up to where you can balance on one leg for up to three minutes.

What are some inexpensive ways to fit physical activity into my day-to-day life?

- Use full water bottles or jugs as dumbbells to do strength-training moves.
- Use a step either indoors or outside to perform step-ups.
- Run or walk up a flight of stairs five to ten times.
- Walk around the field while your kids have sports practice. Ask other moms to walk with you to help the time pass.
- Borrow exercise videos and DVDs from the library or video rental store.
- Take a brisk ten-minute walk during your lunch break.
- Ask coworkers to have walking meetings (where you stroll and talk) rather than long sit-down meetings. (Moving around will also keep everyone feeling alert longer.)

- On cold days, drive to the mall for a brisk indoor walk. (Window-shopping helps the time pass.)

My post-baby belly looks like a kangaroo. What's the best way to improve the look of my stomach bulge?

First of all, know that there's no way to burn fat off of one specific area of the body. However, doing aerobic exercise—like brisk walking, running, stair climbing—in addition to strength training can torch overall body fat, which means it will start melting off your stomach too. You also need to condition the abdominal muscles lying beneath the fat. Start with these three top ab exercises:

Find your foundation. Sitting or standing up straight, draw your belly button in toward your spine and at the same time lift up your pelvic floor. Pause for five seconds. Do two sets of 10 exercises. This helps you access all the deep abdominal muscles that give you the foundation for your core and nice muscle tone. The great thing about this exercise is that you can do it anywhere: while waiting in line at car pool, the grocery store, or bank, or while sitting in a meeting and no one will know!

The bicycle. Lie on your back on the floor with your arms bent and hands behind your head. Bring your left leg toward your right elbow as you twist your upper body to the left. Next, straighten your left leg and bend your right leg, bringing it toward your left elbow as you twist your upper body to the right. Do two sets of twenty.

The Superman. Lie on the floor on your stomach with arms and legs extended straight. At the same time, lift your arms and legs off the floor and hold for ten seconds. Repeat two times.

How do I know if I'm working out hard enough?

Good question! If you're going to spend the time exercising, you might as well get the most out of it. Here are two options.

A *heart-rate monitor.* These used to be expensive gadgets, but today, your options range from low-end versions that just do the basics, like tell time and measure your heart rate, to those with a lot of extra bells and whistles. Here's how to use it:

- As mentioned earlier in the chapter, if you want to burn the most overall fat and calories during a cardio workout, you need to know your resting heart rate and your maximum heart rate. Then you can figure out your optimum workout zone, which is between 60 and 85 percent of that maximum heart rate.

- The most accurate and efficient way to obtain your resting heart rate is first thing in the morning when you wake up after a good night's sleep. Do this before moving around or getting out of bed. Your resting heart rate can rise as you get older and is generally lower in physically fit people. So it's safe to say: the more physically fit you are at any age, the lower your resting heart will be. You can get this heart rate with a heart-rate monitor or by taking your pulse (put your hand on your pulse, count for ten seconds, and multiply by 6 for your beats per minute). The latter isn't as accurate, but it's still a good guide.

- Then use your resting heart rate to calculate your optimum training zone for maximizing both total calories and fat burned in a given workout. The formula for that is:

  220 − your age = your maximum heart rate

Subtract your resting heart rate from your maximum heart rate
which equals your heart rate reserve (HRR)

Multiply your HRR times the percent that you want to train at.

Add back your resting heart rate.

- Below is a sample of the formula that you can use. This is an example of a thirty-two-year-old with a resting heart rate of 68 beats per minute training at a range between 65 and 75 percent.

$220 - 32 = 188$

$188 - 68 = 120$

$120 \text{ x } .65(\%) = 78$

$78 + 68 = 146 \text{ bpm}$

$120 \text{ x } .75(\%) = 90$

$90 + 68 = 158 \text{ bpm}$

- As a result, this thirty-two-year-old's optimum workout zone would be between 146 and 158 beats per minute. As a general recommendation, you will burn more calories and fat overall at the higher intensity levels up to 85 percent max. Unless you are an elite athlete or training for a specific event there is no need and can actually be counterproductive in terms of fat burning to train at levels above 85 percent max for your workouts.

Borg Rating of Perceived Exertion Scale. If you don't have a heart-rate monitor, you can still gauge the intensity of your workout with something called the Borg Rating of Perceived Exertion Scale. (And even if you do have a heart-rate monitor, this is yet another reliable source to gauge your progress from day to day.) It sounds complex, but it's actually pretty simple. Perceived exertion is how hard you think you're working, and as you'll see below, the Borg Scale assigns numbers to different levels of the intensity that you think you're working at.

In order to be in the optimal zone to burn the most overall fat and calories, 65 to 75 percent of your maximum heart rate would roughly correlate with between a 12 to 15 on this scale, and 85 percent of your maximum heart rate would be about 17. Anything above that is likely to be overtraining (not the optimum zone).

Borg Rating of Perceived Exertion Scale

6	No exertion at all
7	Extremely light (7.5)
8	
9	Very light
10	
11	Light
12	
13	Somewhat hard
14	
15	Hard (heavy)
16	
17	Very hard
18	
19	Extremely hard
20	Maximal exertion

Source: Center for Disease Control[6]

3

What's Nutrition Got to Do with It?

I had just finished a grueling workout and was shopping at the drugstore when Jim Hrncir (pronounced "hernsir"), the pharmacist and a family friend, came out.

"Robin, I saw you at the gym this morning and, boy, were you pushing yourself," he said. "You look great."

"I've really been working hard," I said, fishing a box of Hot Tamales candies out of my purse and popping a few in my mouth. "But no matter how hard I work, I just can't get rid of this roll around my middle." I pointed to a fleshy layer of flab that had come on in recent years and stubbornly stayed put on my forty-six-year-old stomach.

"I can tell you exactly why you can't lose that roll," Jim said as he pointed to the candy. "Sugar is like poison to the body, and because the body doesn't know what to do with sugar, it stores it right in the middle." I sheepishly peered into my shopping basket that looked like I was stocking up for Halloween.

"If you eat too much sugar [or other high glycemic index carbohydrates like pasta, white rice, white bread, and potatoes], it causes a spike in insulin, which is a hormone that promotes the transfer of glucose [sugar] from the blood into muscles and other tissues," explained Jim, one of the pioneers of pharmaceutical and nutritional compounding and the owner of Las Colinas Pharmacy Compounding and Wellness Center in Irving, Texas. "After years and years of these insulin spikes, the body finally becomes resistant to the effects of insulin, thus the term 'insulin resistance.' So instead of that sugar being converted into energy, the body stores it as fat, usually around the waistline."

If sugar was poison, then I'd been poisoning myself for years. In fact, I grew up on sugar. When I was young, I'd eat pancakes drenched in syrup or sugary cereal for breakfast and would come home from school to the delicious smell of one of my mother's homemade treats wafting through the air. She had quite a repertoire of cakes, pies, and cookies, and I loved each one more than the next. I preferred dessert over dinner any day. Even as an adult, I went through a period where I could eat sugar all day long. I'd wake up and have a slice of cake with coffee for breakfast. Then while I drove car pool all afternoon, I'd nibble on a roll of Sweet Tarts or bag of gummy candies that I'd polish off by the time I got home. Other times I'd snack on a box of cookies while unpacking the groceries and before I knew it, I'd inhaled half the box! But because I ate an otherwise very healthy diet full of lean protein, produce, and fiber, worked out daily, and had a good metabolism, I didn't gain weight and didn't really think my sweet tooth was a problem.

Years before the day I ran into Jim at the pharmacy, I had given up sugar briefly. The impetus for this was an afternoon in late December when I was home by myself taking down the Christmas decorations. I had my favorite pie—pumpkin—left over from the holidays, so I would alternate packing up ornaments and garlands with eating a bite of pie here and a bite there. By day's end, there was no sign of Christmas in our house and no sign of that pie. I'd eaten the entire thing myself, and truth be told, if I'd had another one, I would have sliced into it too. *This is it,* I thought. *I'm going to make a New Year's resolution not to eat sugar for one year.* As I've said before, the best way for me to achieve a goal is to be accountable, so that night at dinner I announced my intentions to Phillip and the boys. The first few weeks weren't that hard, but as moms of young kids know, avoiding sugar is especially difficult because you're constantly attending birthday parties, postgame ice cream celebrations, and bake sales. With each week that went by, my boys got more and more excited by my willpower and kept cheering me on. There were many times when an intense cookie or licorice craving hit, but I'd think, *how can I cheat when my boys are so proud of me*? I didn't want them to think their mother was a quitter. Amazingly, I made it one whole year without an ounce of sugar passing through my lips. Not a single cookie or cupcake. Not even a peppermint. I felt amazing. I had so much energy, lost weight, and my skin was better. One year to the date, I had a piece of pumpkin pie—and though that time off quelled the intensity of my sweet cravings, boy, did it taste good.

Still, it wasn't until I ran into Jim that I understood *why* sugar was so bad for me. Like I said, I thought it was okay because everything else I was eating was extremely healthy and nutrient-rich, and I was exercising daily and taking really good care of myself. What I didn't realize was that sugar was not only responsible for the roll around my middle, but also for my sometimes flailing energy levels.

"When you first eat it, sugar gives you an initial surge of energy because your blood sugar is spiking, but then it comes down," explains personal trainer and nutritionist Robert Reames. "This quick crash leaves you tired and craving even more sugar to get the lift." This, of course, explains why my morning piece of cake led to midday cookies and then a candy-filled afternoon of car pool. Excess sugar also puts you at risk for weight gain, type 2 diabetes (especially if you have a family history), and an array of diseases like heart disease because it causes insulin levels to rise, which creates inflammation throughout the body. This really stopped me in my tracks because heart disease runs in my family.

And here's another surprising side effect of too much sugar: wrinkles! Yes, it's believed that excess sugar causes a process called glycation. This is when sugar molecules bind to the skin's support structures—collagen and elastin—and break them down. (If I'd known that I would have tossed those Hot Tamales years ago!) The problem is that even if you don't think you have a sweet tooth and don't indulge in the treats that I did, there's sugar hidden in all kinds of foods like jarred pasta sauce, ketchup, yogurt, and breads.

Just look at the labels of some of your favorite foods, and you may be surprised at how much sugar you're consuming. When I saw that one of Phillip's favorite yogurts had 27 grams of sugar in one tiny six-ounce cup I stopped buying it, and now he eats low-fat plain yogurt with fresh berries mixed in. But one reason I think my affair with sugar was truly over the day I saw Jim at the pharmacy was that he told me how sugar can have a negative effect on women going through perimenopause and menopause. At forty-six years old, I'd just started to experience symptoms of this life transition, and anything that could alleviate them was welcomed. Looking back now, I really believe that not eating sugar made my experience with perimenopause and menopause much easier. In fact, I know this is true because the rare times I do indulge my sweet tooth, I often feel the effects. Take a recent week of stressful renovations at my house when I devoured half a cake. Not only did I have the energy highs and lows from spiked blood sugar, but the hot flashes came on like crazy.

Now I'm not saying that sugar is bad for everyone going through peri-menopause or menopause, and someone else may eat bonbons throughout this life transition and feel just fine. Each of us is different, so you need to figure out what works for you. Become your own health detective and write down what you're eating, how you feel, and any symptoms you experience. If you see patterns, you may want to reconsider including certain foods in your diet. Ever since I learned about sugar's impact on the body, I became very interested in nutrition and started reading as much as I could and talking to experts in the field. I also started paying closer attention to what I put into my body and how it reacts, which is exactly why I gave up dairy foods. Several years ago, I realized that every time I ate dairy I'd feel bloated, congested, and lethargic. After a little research, I realized that I had all the symptoms of lactose intolerance. This was bad news for someone like me who loved milk and ice cream, but it wasn't worth how awful I felt after eating it. Besides Greek yogurt and lactose-free cottage cheese, I really cut back on dairy foods.

That said, I know how important it is for women to consume enough calcium in order to help build strong, dense bones and prevent osteoporosis, a disease in which bones become fragile and weak, increasing their risk of fracturing and breaking. (Women are four times more likely to suffer from this disease than men![1]) Calcium also helps muscles to contract, blood to clot, and your nerves to send messages to the rest of your body. "A woman's body starts losing calcium in her midtwenties and if she doesn't get enough, by the time she's fifty years old, she may have low bone mineral density, a condition called osteopenia, which is a precursor to osteoporosis," Jim explains. At the same time, you need vitamin D, which helps your body absorb calcium (it's also believed to have a strong anti-inflammatory effect on the body, which may decrease your risk of diseases like breast cancer and heart disease). Since I limit dairy in my diet, I make sure to get the calcium I need with a good supplement that also contains vitamin D3. Experts say it's best to get calcium from foods. "But if you're going to take a supplement there are different types and some are more or less beneficial," Jim adds. "I suggest a type of calcium supplement called MCHC, which contains all the micronutrients you need to absorb the calcium like magnesium and boron as well as vitamin D3." The recommendation is 1,000 milligrams (mg) of calcium and 400–800 IU of vitamin D for women ages nineteen to forty-nine and 1,200 mg of calcium and 800–1000 IU of vitamin D for women over age fifty, according to the National Osteoporosis Foundation.[2]

Paying attention to my body also taught me that sometimes a food you could eat freely when you were younger doesn't agree with you as you get older. For me, that happened with peanut butter. Growing up, my mother would serve it on sandwiches, with bananas, or put it on celery. When I was pregnant with Jay, I'd put it on pancakes. When I was pregnant with Jordan, Phillip would toast four slices of bread at a time, spread them with peanut butter, and then while I was devouring that, he'd make me two more pieces. My passion for peanut butter went in phases, so I'd been off it for a while when we first moved to California. There I discovered a new favorite snack: fresh blueberry bagels from a local bakery topped with peanut butter. Just the thought of them gets my mouth watering, but after a few weeks of eating that daily, I realized that I got that same bloated, sluggish feeling I got from dairy. During an allergy test, I learned that I can't digest peanut butter, and so for the sake of my distended stomach and energy level, I've totally given it up. Yes, I miss it a lot, but again it's not worth the post-peanut butter discomfort that lasted much longer than the actual snack.

Robin's Rx Here are some healthy cooking tips that I learned from my friend executive chef Dora Cordts:

- Use Greek yogurt instead of heavy cream or sour cream in recipes. Greek yogurt is a natural probiotic, a good bacteria that helps maintain the health of your gastrointestinal tract and boosts your immune system. It's also easier to digest and lower in fat and calories than heavy or sour cream.
- Instead of risotto, use faro, a high-protein whole grain that tastes delicious and fills you up.
- Buy fresh uncooked flour tortillas instead of the traditional precooked packaged ones and bake them instead of frying. (They also make great baked chips.) Uncooked tortillas are typically made with canola oil instead of lard and are lower in saturated fat.

Besides avoiding foods that make me physically sick, I don't limit what I eat. I don't diet and never have in my life. I believe that's why my metabolism is healthily humming along at the age of fifty-five. It's why I've never been five pounds over the weight I am now (besides when I was pregnant and shortly thereafter) and why I didn't battle my weight during menopause like many women do. I watch what I eat (except on vacation), but I don't deny myself.

I often get letters from young women asking for advice on staying or getting trim, and the best thing I can tell them is: never starve yourself. At twenty and thirty years old you have a healthy metabolism, but you can change all that with crash dieting or starving yourself. "When your body is deprived of calories, it starts storing fat and breaking down lean muscle to get energy," explains Robert Reames. "With less muscle, you slow down your metabolism." Even when I had eighty pounds to lose after Jay was born, I didn't diet; I lost the weight by eating.

Initially, I wasn't focused on the weight at all. I was getting used to life with a newborn, and then at two weeks old, Jay had to have emergency surgery for a digestive disorder known as pyloric stenosis. As you can imagine, after that I was so incredibly relieved and thankful that Jay was healthy that the last thing I cared about was the size of my thighs. Instead, I was enjoying every wonderful and overwhelming minute of new motherhood. Every night, when I'd hear Jay cry for his 2:00 a.m. feeding, I had a routine. I'd walk into the kitchen and preheat the oven before going to Jay's room to change his diaper. Then I'd carry him back to the kitchen, toss six pieces of Mrs. GoodCookie cookie dough in the oven, and warm his bottle. By the time his bottle was warm, my cookies were ready and I'd carry them and Jay into the den and turn on my favorite Anne Murray CD. Just thinking of those nights gives me chills because they were truly some of my happiest times. There I'd sit, surrounded by that still quiet you only experience in the middle of the night, and cradling Jay's warm little body in my arms while Anne Murray sang softly in the background. There were no phones or doorbell ringing and no surprise guests popping by. It was just the two of us, and it felt magical. (And of course, having fresh, hot cookies didn't hurt.) I was in such bliss that I didn't notice or care about the extra weight I was carrying around on my 5 foot 3 inches frame.

That was until one day around six weeks postpartum, when I went to the grocery store. The manager, an old friend, saw me and came over to say hi. "Robin, when are you finally going to have that baby?" he asked.

My heart sank. "I had him six weeks ago," I said. I was mortified, but it was just the inspiration I needed to cancel my nightly meetings with Mrs. GoodCookie and do something to slim down and feel better about myself. Truth be told, though the cookies were delicious, they made it hard to go back to sleep and I often woke up feeling sluggish and bloated. And wearing my maternity clothes six weeks postpartum did little for my self-esteem.

With my doctor's okay, I set out to lose the weight. At his suggestion, I'd start the day with a cup of apple cider vinegar mixed with one cup of warm water and one to two tablespoons concentrated lemon juice, which he said would help detox my body and jump-start my metabolism. This combo also helps with fluid retention, which is why I still drink it today. After that, I'd roast a turkey breast and put it in the refrigerator. Every time I got hungry, I'd slice off some turkey and roll it up with a thin slice of cheese and a pickle. I ate the same thing for dinner, but added cottage cheese with red vinegar dressing and chopped up cucumbers. Less than three months after that mortifying moment in the supermarket, I was happily back to my prepregnancy weight.

Robin's Rx I was intrigued to learn that what you eat or drink before bed can affect how you sleep. "You may think that alcohol will help you sleep, but it actually prevents you from getting into the most restorative stages of sleep and can wake you up during the night," says Frank Lawlis, PhD, psychologist, researcher, and author of *The Stress Answer* and *The IQ Answer.* "On the other hand, foods that stimulate the production of serotonin, a relaxing brain chemical, can help you sleep. Examples include milk, mild cheese, watermelon, ham, turkey, and almonds." Just make sure these pre-bed snacks are small, because trying to digest a big meal can keep you up. Also, if you're one of those people who gets wired from caffeine, stop drinking it in the early afternoon; otherwise, it may stay in your system, leaving you wide-eyed come bedtime.

I ate all day long back then, and I still do today—about every two hours. I think most people would be shocked to see how much I eat. In fact, despite thirty-five years together, there are times when even Phillip is amazed by it. (He lovingly calls me a "chowhound," a nickname I find endearing.) I'm simply not your dressing-on-the-side or steamed-veggies-only kind of girl. And I never want to be. Food is too delicious and life is too short to deprive yourself of all the yummy tastes out there. (I also think I'd be an absolute witch to live with if I couldn't eat.) My feeling is if you really enjoy your meals, you're more satisfied. It's when you deprive yourself that you're constantly hungry and thinking about food.

And here's something that may surprise you: I eat carbs. And I eat them every day! I simply couldn't live in a low-carb world—especially because sandwiches are my favorite food. Though I like traditional BLTs or tuna fish, I also get creative with my sandwiches. One of my favorites is Ezekiel bread, lactose-free cream cheese, alfalfa sprouts, tomatoes, cucumbers, avocado, and pickles. I try to make sure that most of the breads I choose are rich in fiber (a nutrient that helps with constipation and may help protect against diseases like colon cancer). "Also, carbs are the body's main energy source, and if you don't get enough, your body will break down muscle to get that energy," Robert explains. They also stimulate your brain's production of serotonin, a chemical that helps you feel calm and de-stressed.

However, Robert has taught me that all carbs are not created equal. Those that have little to no fiber, like refined pasta, white rice, and white bread, don't offer these benefits. But complex carbs like brown and wild rice, potatoes with skin, and high-fiber cereal and bread give you the stamina you need to get through your busy day. "Fiber also makes you feel fuller faster and for a longer period of time. Additionally, it keeps blood sugar levels balanced, which helps curb cravings for processed sugars and carbs like candy, cake, and cookies," says Robert. (This is why I ate a lot of fiber when I was trying to kick my sugar habit.)

You can also find fiber in fruits and vegetables along with an array of important nutrients called antioxidants that not only protect against cancer and heart problems, but protect skin cells from breaking down. I start my day with a cup of cut-up papaya, which contains important digestive enzymes and nutrients that are good for the skin. I eat this on the way to the studio, and then later in the morning I snack on sliced apples with walnuts or blueberries mixed with cottage cheese. I also love watermelon (which was a staple in my diet while pregnant with Jordan) because it's thirst-quenching, filling, and contains lycopene, a powerful antioxidant also found in tomato sauce and grapefruits. I also love vegetables, so I have no problem getting the recommended five to nine servings a day. I eat at least one big salad per day and snack on green beans, snap peas, and my all-time favorite: raw cucumber chopped up in tuna and chicken salad. Cruciferous veggies, which include cabbage, kale, cauliflower, and broccoli, are foods I ate a lot of when I was going through menopause because they provide a natural way to slow down the formation and circulation of certain estrogens.

> **Robin's Rx** Eat raw fruits and vegetables like apples, carrots, and pears not only because they can help prevent disease, but because they can help whiten your teeth. Their hard texture rubbing up against teeth can physically remove some stain-causing particles. Since these foods require so much chewing, they stimulate saliva flow, which helps rinse stains away.

My other favorite food group is protein, an important nutrient to help our muscles, tissues, organs, cells, and bones grow and repair themselves. It's also a critical component of collagen, the structure in our skin that keeps it firm, so in a sense eating protein may help you look younger. I like turkey and chicken, but my favorites are red meat like prime rib and rib eye steaks. (I guess you can take the girl out of Texas, but you can't take the Texas out of the girl.) I try to pick the pieces of meat that are lowest in fat (the ones with the least amount of marbling) and trim any excess fat when I get home.

Though I'm fine with a little salmon every once in a while, I'm not a big fan of fish. I wish I were, because fish is not only a great source of protein, but it contains essential fatty acids like omega-3s, which can help reduce inflammation throughout the body (which affects aging), lower cholesterol, and protect against an array of diseases from heart disease to depression. Omega-3s are especially important if you're pregnant or breast-feeding, since research shows that they help in the development of the baby's brain and nervous system. Lastly, these essential fatty acids can also keep your skin looking plump and hydrated. Though I don't eat fish, I get my fill of omega-3s by eating flax seeds, walnuts, pumpkin seeds, and eggs that are fortified with them and by taking fish oil supplements. I also make sure that Phillip and I eat other healthy fats like real butter, olive oil, virgin coconut oil, and avocado, which are good for your body as well as keeping hair, skin, and nails looking healthy. We also try hard to avoid trans fats, which are manmade chemicals used to give food a longer shelf life. You can find them in full-fat dairy products, processed meats like ham, and packaged foods like cakes and cookies. Luckily, with all the negative attention these fats are getting, a lot of companies are taking trans fats out of their foods or reporting them on their labels.

I know it can seem overwhelming to try to eat healthy or slim down, but here are some tips that help me eat and live this way every day.

Never skip breakfast. This first meal is what gives your metabolism a kickstart for the day. Your body has already fasted for at least eight hours while you were sleeping, so if you don't eat breakfast it can go into starvation mode. Also, go all morning without eating anything, and you'll likely find that you're so hungry by lunch that your healthy-eating intentions for the day fly right out the window. But you can't just eat anything for breakfast. Foods high in fat and sugar, like doughnuts, pastries, and muffins, will cause a spike in blood sugar followed by an energy crash and won't keep you full until lunch. Robert says the most filling breakfasts are those that are low in sugar and combine protein and carbs, like high-fiber cereal with berries and low-fat milk or an egg and toast.

Plan your meals. This is key for busy women, because if you don't plan or have snacks with you, you'll get hungry and stop at the first fast-food drive-through you see. It helps to figure out a week's worth of menus—or at least what you're going to eat tomorrow—make a list of all the foods that you need for the week, and go shopping so you have all the ingredients on hand at all times. One way I make sure that most of my meals are healthy is to bring my own food to the studio, like cut-up fruit, Greek yogurt, Ezekiel bread, sunflower seeds, and cottage cheese.

Robin's Way

Typical day:

Breakfast: coffee, cut-up papaya, poached egg on a piece of Ezekiel toast with butter, low-fat biscuit or whole-wheat pancakes

Midmorning Snack: sliced apple with walnuts or almonds big bowl of low-fat, lactose-free cottage cheese with blueberries and sunflower seeds

Lunch: turkey or chicken sandwich

Midafternoon Snack: toast with honey or sliced apple with walnuts and turkey.

Dinner: chicken or steak, scooped-out baked potato with a little mustard, and salad

Pre-Bed Snack: small container of Greek yogurt

Keep a food diary. For me, being accountable really helps me stay on a healthy eating track, and a food diary is a great way to do just that. Though I don't keep a food log, I have many friends who swear by it, and research confirms this. A recent study of almost two thousand people at Kaiser Permanente's Center for Health Research in Portland, Oregon, found that those who wrote down what they ate each day lost twice as much weight as those who didn't.[3] You can keep your log on a plain notepad or your computer or PDA. I know people who e-mail their food diaries to a weight-loss buddy (talk about being accountable). What method you use to write down your food doesn't matter as long as you use it.

Choose smaller dishes. The average dinner plate has gone from nine inches in diameter to over twelve inches the last twenty years, and most of us fill our plates until there's no room left. After all, nothing says deprivation more than a tiny amount of food floating on a large, empty plate. A great trick is to serve yourself meals on salad-sized plates and in small bowls. This way you eat smaller portions, but your plate looks full so you trick your brain and don't feel deprived.

Make healthy substitutions. Did you know that one bagel is the caloric equivalent of at least three slices of bread? When I heard that I almost fell over and right then and there decided to limit how often I ate bagels. For less than half the calories, you can have an English muffin. Other good substitutions: instead of mayonnaise, try mustard or even use mashed avocado as a spread and get all those heart-healthy omega-3s. Switch from regular milk to low-fat or skim milk and full fat yogurt to the low-fat variety.

Robin's Rx Here's a healthy way to make potato skins without all the fat and calories of the traditional version. Bake a potato and then scoop out most of the filling (but do leave just a little bit). Then spread it with mustard, a dash of picante sauce, or nonfat cream cheese. It tastes so good and provides you with important nutrients like potassium, vitamin C, vitamin B6, and fiber.

Read food labels. Most packages carry a "Nutrition Facts" section, which tells you how much fat, fiber, protein, sugar, and calories, among other nutrients, are in a particular food. It also tells you how much of that food equals a serving. This can be really helpful if you're trying to watch your weight. I remember a friend who was trying to lose weight but couldn't understand why her scale wouldn't budge. The nutrition facts label on her favorite chips said that a serving was 140 calories. She'd eat the whole bag thinking she'd only consumed 140 calories. That was until she took a closer look and saw that there were fourteen servings in that bag, a total of almost 2,000 calories!

Drink enough water. Water hydrates our organs and skin and helps flush toxins out of the body. I was in my thirties when a trainer at the gym told me this, so I started drinking several bottles a day. I immediately dropped a couple of pounds—and when you're 5 foot 3 inches a couple of pounds is like ten pounds—and my skin looked clear and fresh. Though the recommended amount is eight 8-ounce glasses a day, I need to drink more than that on days when I exercise because I sweat so much. Water is also important if you're trying to lose weight, because it fills you up and the only way you're going to get rid of the fat you've burned while exercising is through your urine. To keep water from being boring, I add healthy flavor with Janet Skin Care Hydro Tea Facial Feed, drops of green tea that come in peach, passion fruit, and mint flavors. They don't have any calories, but they're full of amazing nutrients that rev up your metabolism and protective antioxidants.

Flush yourself out. I have struggled with water retention my whole life, so I make sure to eat foods that are natural diuretics (meaning they help remove extra water from the body). These include grapefruit, watermelon, asparagus, celery, and cucumbers. I also take garlic papaya capsules, a natural diuretic that prevents water retention without depleting my body of the potassium.

Sip green tea. Not only is the whole act of brewing, steeping, and sipping tea relaxing, but an endless array of studies point out a long list of health benefits associated with green tea, which is made with pure tea leaves that haven't had much processing. One recent study out of Athens Medical School in Greece found that green tea may improve how the cells that line our circulatory systems function, which may help protect against heart disease.[4]

Skip the soda. I never even tried soda until I was almost grown (we were so poor that the rare times we went out to eat burgers, we couldn't afford fries *and* a soda). But I've been addicted to Tab for thirty years. I used to have two to three a day, and then I cut down to one every few days. That was until I was doing research for this book and found out how bad diet sodas are for you. They contain phosphoric and citric acids, and many experts think their artificial sweeteners may cause health problems. Plus, results from a study done at the USDA Human Nutrition Research Center on Aging at Tufts University found that the more cola women drank, the lower their bone mineral density.[5] A second study from the University of Texas Health Science Center found that people who drank diet soda were 65 percent more likely to become overweight during the next seven to eight years than those who didn't drink soda.[6] If all that's not enough to make you put down that cola can, I don't know what is!

Now, I just want to say that despite my interest in nutrition and caring deeply about what I put into my body, my diet is in no way perfect. Of course, there are times when I really want a bowl of ice cream or a big, heaping spoonful of homemade whipped cream. Before I indulge, I ask myself, "Do I want the instant gratification from this food?" or "Do I want to spend all day feeling bloated, congested, and irritable?" Though at times the latter is enough to stop me in my tracks, other times I go ahead and eat the ice cream or whipped cream despite the consequences. Even sugar has an occasional place in my diet. I don't eat a lot of it, but I love birthday and wedding cake; and if it's someone's birthday or wedding, I'm the first in line for dessert. Or if one weekend I happen to eat six cinnamon rolls (which I did recently), I eat them and enjoy every sugary bite without regret. What's the point of eating them if you're going to spend the rest of the day beating yourself up? I just balance myself by having a light dinner that night and flushing my body with lots of water. And then I move on. I know that I work out hard, take good care of myself, and that an indulgence here or there is healthy for the body and soul.

Answers from the Expert

Robert Reames, CSCS, D, CN, RTS1, CPT, personal trainer and nutritionist, official trainer and nutritionist for the Dr. Phil Ultimate Weight Loss Challenge, author of *Make Over Your Metabolism,* and creator of the Robert Reames Lifestyle Transformation System DVD series.

What are antioxidants, and why are they so important?

Throughout the course of a day, our bodies are attacked by compounds in our environment called free radicals, which can destroy cells throughout the body causing diseases and aging. Antioxidants act as an army that battles these free radicals in order to keep you healthy and reduce dangerous inflammation in the body. They're also believed to help skin stay firm. This all may sound very technical, but getting antioxidants in your diet is easy if you aim to eat the recommended five to nine servings of fruits and vegetables daily. Though most of them have antioxidants, some of the best sources include blueberries, pomegranates, cranberries, cherries, raspberries, apples, and black beans. Newer foods that you may hear about are acai and goji berries, which contain high concentrations of antioxidants as well as other nutrients.

I'm trying to lose weight and often get hungry between meals. What are the best snacks to keep my hand out of the cookie jar?

Ideally, a snack will suppress hunger with a combination of protein and fiber but doesn't have more than 100–200 calories. Both nutrients slow the digestive process, which keeps you feeling full longer, and recent research shows that protein suppresses ghrelin, a hormone secreted by the stomach that stimulates appetite. Good snacks are an apple or orange with a handful of almonds or walnuts, or low-fat cheese sticks with a piece of fruit or sliced veggies with hummus.

What can I do today to clean up my diet and improve my eating habits?

The most important thing to do is to control your environment so it does not control you. Clean all unhealthy, high-fat, and high-sugar junk foods, snacks, and cereal out of your cabinets and refrigerator. This way if a late-night chocolate craving hits, you can't indulge it, because you can't eat what's not there. If you can't completely clear out the kitchen because other family members eat these foods, at least put them in a separate cabinet or shelf that you can't see.

Here are some other tips:

- Stock up on good-for-you foods like fresh or frozen fruits and vegetables, canned beans, fiber-rich breads, and lean protein. Set yourself up for success by having these foods in clear view. For example, place a big bowl of fruit on the counter and cut-up fruits and veggies at eye level in the fridge.
- Brown-bag your lunch. If you bring your own food to work or when you're out with your kids, you can better control portion sizes, fat, and calories than you can if you go to a restaurant or the office cafeteria. (Added bonus: you'll save money too.)
- Have emergency foods stashed everywhere from your office to your car to your purse. Oatmeal packets, string cheese, portable fruits like apples and bananas, nuts, and yogurt are good choices.
- Don't be fooled by foods that are labeled "fat free." Often they're no lower in calories because the fat is replaced with loads and loads of sugar. If you do choose to eat these foods, at least make sure to measure out a serving.
- Find ways to soothe your stress. A lot of times, stress-related snacking causes us to consume sugar and fat-laden foods. Instead of eating

when you're feeling upset or anxious, take a walk (even if it's just around the block), call a close friend, take a bath, or do anything else that's non-food-related and soothing to you. Make a list of these things when you're in a calm state of mind and keep it handy.

For a couple of days, write down everything you normally eat. (Most people are surprised to see how much they consume and that they do so even when they're not hungry.) After a few days, take a look and find places where you can tweak your diet in a healthy way. For example, you can eat yogurt for a snack instead of cookies or have an open-faced sandwich instead of two pieces of bread.

- Control your portions. Often it's not *what* we're eating that makes us gain weight; it's how much we're eating. Divide large boxes of cereal and snack foods into serving size bags to prevent overeating. Research shows that we tend to eat more from a large bag than a smaller one. Also, use measuring cups and spoons to make sure you're eating an appropriate serving size (eventually you'll be able to know what a serving is just by looking at it).

- Slow down. It takes a good twenty minutes for our stomachs to tell our brains we're full. That means if you rush through your meal, you may eat much more food than you actually need to be satisfied. Instead, eat slowly, putting your fork down between bites. Pay attention to the act of chewing and tasting your food (rather than multitasking by eating while watching TV, checking e-mail, or doing work).

- Learn from difficult moments. Being able to recover from setbacks is critical in all areas of your life. And healthy eating and weight loss are no different. Just because you ate a few slices of cake too many or finished that bag of chips doesn't mean you should give up on your plan to eat healthy. Instead, figure out what happened and use this information in the future. Next time you have a stressful work project to complete, bring good-for-you snacks like soy chips or cut-up fruit rather than potato chips; or next time you go to a party, eat a piece of fruit beforehand so you're not hungry when you arrive.

- Accentuate the positive. Instead of thinking about all the things you shouldn't eat, focus on the amazing and delicious healthy foods you *can* eat. Once you start looking for healthy options, you'll see how many there are and how good they can taste. Check out low-fat, low-calorie cookbooks and regularly try new fruits and vegetables you see in the produce aisle rather than sticking with the same apple, banana, and carrots that you always eat.

- Educate yourself. Expand your knowledge of nutrition and living a healthy lifestyle by reading books and articles on these subjects.

I don't have the money to buy healthy foods. What can I do?

You don't have to be rich to eat foods that are good for you; you just need to plan ahead. Take one day a week to cook inexpensive, healthy meals in bulk such as soups, brown rice, beans, and grilled chicken and then store the extras in the freezer. Always buy whatever produce is in season, since it's usually less expensive, and if fresh fruits and vegetables aren't in your budget, buy the frozen variety (which studies show are just as nutritious).

I don't know how to order something healthy when I go to a restaurant. Any tips?

Portions at restaurants are huge, so try ordering an appetizer instead of a full entrée, splitting a meal with a friend, or cutting the entrée in half as soon as it comes to the table and asking for one half to be packed up. Don't be afraid to ask how foods are prepared and request things like dressing on the side, a salad or vegetables in the place of french fries, or for the chef to use little oil when preparing your dish. If you're going to a restaurant that's part of a chain, often you can check their menus and nutritional information on the Web site. This way you can choose something healthy in advance and not be tempted by a huge menu and delicious smells when you're hungry. Lastly, one foolproof way to avoid a high-calorie catastrophe: don't order anything with the words *deep fried* or *fried* in front of it. Better choices are foods that are grilled or steamed.

Can eating late at night make you gain weight?

That depends on a couple of things. If you skip meals throughout the day and then think that gives you license to "make up for it" or "reward yourself for the day" with a big meal at night, then yes, you will gain weight. Having said that, if you're eating consistently nutritious meals throughout the day, you won't be hungry late at night and won't have the tendency to overeat. My overall recommendation would be not to have a heavy meal directly before bed. You want to be resting well throughout the night, not digesting. Also don't exceed the twelve- to sixteen-hour time period between your last meal for the day and breakfast the next morning. Going without a meal for that long will begin to put your body in fat storage mode, where it is breaking down lean muscle (which you want to build and keep!) for energy, which will overall lower your metabolism.

Is it true that not getting enough sleep can make you fat?

Yes and there are several suspected reasons why sleep deprivation can lead to weight gain.

- When you sleep, your body releases growth hormone, which helps you release energy from your fat cells, and leptin, a hormone that regulates your appetite and lets you know that you're full. If you're not sleeping, that means your body decreases the production of these hormones. In turn, this may increase your chances of gaining weight.

- On the other hand, lack of sleep may boost the production of another hormone called ghrelin, which actually increases your appetite, and the stress hormone cortisol, which can negatively impact your metabolism and promote insulin resistance. As mentioned earlier in the chapter, insulin resistance can cause you to gain weight, especially around the middle.

- If you're sleep deprived, you're usually tired; and being tired often leads to overeating—especially high-refined sugar and carbohydrates or salty, fatty foods.

What exactly should I eat to lose weight and get healthy?

Diets don't work, so it's important to make a commitment to a lifestyle that is going to support healthy eating. For Dr. Phil's Ultimate Weight Loss Challenge, the participants got a kick-start by following the fourteen-day Rapid Start Plan from Dr. Phil's book *The Ultimate Weight Solution Food Guide.*[7] It's not a diet, but rather an example of a healthy way to eat and a good guide in terms of the kinds of foods you want to include in your diet. After two weeks of this plan, you'll have a better sense of portion size and how to make sure meals are nutritionally balanced. Also, if you're trying to slim down, sometimes it helps to start with a preplanned menu so you don't have to think about what you'll eat and you get used to new eating habits. Each meal combines protein, carbs, and fat, while being low in sugar, salt, fat, and cholesterol.

Day 1
Breakfast

    1 serving of high fiber cereal (e.g. All-Bran, Bran Buds, Fruit & Fiber,
      or Fiber One)
    1 cup low-fat skim or soy milk

1 egg, scrambled (or two egg whites, scrambled)
Strawberries (or other seasonal fruit)
Coffee or tea

Snack

Pear

Lunch

Water-packed tuna with 1 sliced tomato served on a generous bed of
lettuce, chopped green peppers, radishes, and other salad
vegetables
2 tablespoons low-calorie Italian salad dressing

Snack

1 cup low-fat, sugar-free plain yogurt mixed with 1 tablespoon
sugar-free apricot preserves

Dinner

Roasted chicken breast
Asparagus spears, steamed or boiled
Summer squash, steamed or boiled

Day 2
Breakfast

Turkey breakfast sausage, 2 links
Oat bran cereal, cooked
½ grapefruit
Coffee or tea

Snack

Banana smoothie: 1 frozen banana blended with 1 cup low-fat milk
or soy milk

Lunch

Mediterranean salad: ½ cup garbanzo beans on generous bed of
mixed greens and chopped salad vegetables
1 tablespoon olive oil mixed with balsamic vinegar to taste

Snack

1 cup low-fat, sugar-free yogurt (any flavor)

Dinner

Grilled salmon
Broccoli, steamed or boiled
Carrots, cooked

Day 3

Breakfast

Fat-free ham, 2 slices
Low-fat granola mixed with 1 cup low-fat, sugar-free yogurt (any flavor)
1 orange
Coffee or tea

Snack

Apple

Lunch

Chicken Caesar salad: cubed grilled chicken breast, shredded
Romaine lettuce, with an assortment of other chopped salad
vegetables, 2 tablespoons reduced-fat Caesar salad dressing

Snack

½ cup low-fat cottage cheese with baby carrots and other cut-up raw
vegetables

Dinner

Beef tenderloin
Green peas, boiled
Cauliflower, steamed or boiled

Day 4
Breakfast

1 egg, scrambled
Oatmeal, cooked
1 cup low-fat, skim or soy milk
Cantaloupe (or other seasonal fruit)
Coffee or tea

Snack

Fresh berries

Lunch

Black bean chili: ½ cup cooked black beans, 2 tablespoons salsa, 2
tablespoons chopped onions, ½ cup stewed tomatoes

Snack

1 cup low-fat, sugar-free yogurt (any flavor)

Dinner

Roasted turkey breast
Brussels sprouts, steamed or boiled
Tossed salad
2 tablespoons low-fat French salad dressing

Day 5

Breakfast

2 egg whites, scrambled
1 serving high-fiber cereal
1 cup low-fat, skim or soy milk
Raspberries (or other seasonal fruit)
Coffee or tea

Snack

Cut up assorted raw vegetables
1 ounce reduced-fat Swiss cheese

Lunch

Grilled chicken breast
Shredded cabbage tossed with 2 tablespoons low-fat coleslaw
    dressing

Snack

Pear

Dinner

Baked Cornish game hen
Carrots, cooked
Kale, cooked

Day 6

Breakfast

Turkey bacon, 2 slices
Oat bran cereal, cooked
Nectarine or peach
Coffee or tea

Snack

1 cup low-fat sugar-free yogurt (any flavor)

Lunch

Broiled hamburger patty, extra lean
Tossed salad
2 tablespoons low-fat salad dressing
1 cup raw grapes

Snack

½ cup low-fat cottage cheese with cut-up raw vegetables

Dinner

Baked cod or other whitefish
French-style green beans, boiled
Yellow squash, steamed or boiled

Day 7

Breakfast

1 egg, scrambled
Corn grits, cooked
Honeydew melon
Coffee or tea

Snack

Apple

Lunch

Cooked eggplant topped with ½ cup tomato sauce, ½ cup cubed tofu,
and 1 ounce of grated fat-free Mozzarella cheese
Tossed salad with 1 tablespoon olive oil and balsamic vinegar

Snack

1 cup plain low-fat, sugar-free yogurt with 1 tablespoon sugar-free
strawberry preserves

Dinner

Roasted pork tenderloin
Cabbage, boiled
Okra slices, boiled

Day 8
Breakfast

Turkey sausage, 2 links
1 serving high-fiber cereal
1 cup low-fat skim or soy milk
½ grapefruit
Coffee or tea

Snack

Sliced cucumbers dipped in ½ cup low-fat cottage cheese

Lunch

Vegetarian lunch: ½ cup kidney beans topped with 2 tablespoons salsa
Artichoke, steamed, leaves dipped in 2 tablespoons low-fat Italian dressing
Raw baby carrots

Snack

Pear

Dinner

Eye of the round
Tomatoes, stewed
Cauliflower, steamed or boiled

Day 9
Breakfast

Turkey bacon, 2 slices
Smoothie: Blend 1 cup low-fat, skim or soy milk with berries
Coffee or tea

Snack

Apple

Lunch

Broiled hamburger patty, extra lean
Spinach salad: chopped fresh spinach, ½ cup white beans,
    2 tablespoons chopped onion, 2 tablespoons chopped red pepper
    and 1 tablespoon olive oil with balsamic vinegar to taste

Snack

1 cup low-fat sugar-free yogurt (any flavor)

Dinner

Baked chicken breast
Yellow snap beans, boiled
Fresh tomato, sliced

Day 10
Breakfast

2 egg whites, scrambled
Shredded wheat
1 cup low-fat, skim or soy milk
Banana, sliced
Coffee or tea

Snack

Plum

Lunch

Three bean salad: ¼ cup garbanzo beans, ¼ cup kidney beans, ½ cup cooked green beans, 2 tablespoons chopped onion, 2 tablespoons chopped roasted red peppers, and 2 tablespoons low-fat Italian dressing—served on a bed of Romaine lettuce

Snack

1 cup low-fat, sugar-free yogurt (any flavor)

Dinner

Steamed Alaskan king crab
Mixed vegetables, steamed (broccoli, zucchini, yellow squash)

Day 11
Breakfast

1 egg, poached
Oatmeal, cooked
Orange
Coffee or tea

Snack

Fruit smoothie: 1 cup low-fat, skim or soy milk blended with berries

Lunch

Ground turkey, lean, broiled or grilled
Grilled portabella mushroom
Fresh tomato, sliced, topped with 1 ounce reduced-fat feta cheese

Snack

Cut-up raw vegetables

Dinner

Grilled salmon
Broccoli and cauliflower medley, steamed
Tossed salad with 1 tablespoon olive oil

Day 12

Breakfast

Turkey sausage, 2 links
1 serving high-fiber cereal
1 cup low-fat, skim or soy milk
Raspberries (or other seasonal fruit)
Coffee or tea

Snack

Pear

Lunch

Spinach and shrimp salad: cooked shrimp, 2 tablespoons chopped
onion, 1 sliced tomato, raw spinach, and 2 tablespoons low-fat
mayonnaise

Snack

Cut-up raw vegetables dipped in ½ cup low-fat cottage cheese

Dinner

Grilled sirloin steak
Broccoli, steamed
Yellow squash, steamed or boiled

Day 13
Breakfast

2 egg whites, scrambled
Cream of Wheat cereal
1 cup melon balls (or other seasonal fruit)
Coffee or tea

Snack

Orange

Lunch

Low-fat chef salad: 2 slices reduced-fat ham, 1 ounce low-fat/low-sodium cheddar cheese, chopped lettuce and assorted cut-up salad vegetables, 2 tablespoons low-fat French dressing

Snack

1 cup low-fat, sugar-free yogurt (any flavor)

Dinner

Grilled tuna steak
Yellow snap beans, steamed or boiled
Asparagus, steamed or boiled

Day 14
Breakfast

Turkey sausages, 2 links
1 serving high-fiber cereal
1 cup low-fat, skim or soy milk
Sliced peaches
Coffee or tea

Snack

1 cup low-fat, sugar-free yogurt (any flavor)

Lunch

Grilled chicken breast
French-style green beans, boiled
Baked potato, medium

Snack

Banana

Dinner

Roast beef
Stewed tomatoes
Tossed salad with 2 tablespoons low-fat blue cheese dressing

What's Skin Care Got to Do with It?

There I was in my usual seat at a recent taping of the show when I felt a gentle tap on my shoulder. When I turned around, a very well-dressed, fifty-something woman behind me leaned over and whispered conspiratorially in my ear, "Robin, I've been sitting behind you all morning. There's something I just can't figure out and it's driving me nuts!" she said. From her vantage point, all she could see was the back of my hair, so I hadn't a clue what she was going to say. "I've been looking at the side of your face and back of your ears for the entire show, and I can't see your scars," she continued. "You have the best plastic surgeon in town! Can I have his number?" This wasn't the first time that I'd heard this comment or some variation of it.

While I've done a lot of things to maintain the firmness of my face, which we'll talk about shortly, going under the knife isn't one of them. I'm a very open person and not shy about telling it like it is (guess it runs in the family), so I'd admit it if I'd had a face-lift—especially after the endless queries I've received on the subject. I also haven't had any other complexion-smoothing surgeries be it a mid-face-lift, lower-lift, or mini-lift. (Truth be told, if I were going to lift something, it would be my breasts first, and butt second.) I read all the time where people say that I look plastic, and all I can say is that's just the way I look and always have. There's a cute scene in the movie *The Women* where Annette Bening's character is walking through a department store and a salesperson from one of the cosmetic counters asks her, "Would you like a face-lift in a bottle?" Annette Bening says something like, "This is my face. Get over it." I love that scene and her attitude because it's exactly the way I feel.

Of course, just because I haven't had a face-lift doesn't mean that I haven't thought about it. After all, I don't think I'm perfect by any means and, like most women, I've had those moments when I look in the mirror and see a line or skin sagging that wasn't there the day before. In my early forties, I was at a Dallas beauty salon when I ran into a female acquaintance who looked absolutely gorgeous. She'd always been attractive, but her lined and weathered complexion made her seem older than her fifty-three years. Since I'd last seen her, she'd had a face-lift that left her looking like herself, just more refreshed and youthful. I made a mental note that fifty-three must be the right age to have a face-lift and that I'd investigate when the time came. Then several things happened. As time passed, I knew more and more people who'd had plastic surgery with less than stellar results and heard stories of surgeries gone awry. I know that those incidences are the exception more than the rule and that, for the most part, if you see a reputable and board-certified surgeon you'll be okay. But, I wondered, what if I were the one to have the doctor sneeze midsurgery, slip, and cut off my nose or sever a facial nerve, leaving half my face paralyzed? Statistically, there's a small chance of a negative outcome, but that's not the least bit comforting if you're one of those women it happens to.

On a less serious note, what if I simply didn't like how I looked after going through all that pain and recovery? One of my goals in life is to never live with regret in any area, yet there are no guarantees with plastic surgery. Post-op, it's too late to get your old face back. The final straw? One night while flipping the TV channels, I stumbled on a medical program where they were showing an actual face-lift operation. I just about fainted when I saw the doctor put his hand inside this woman's cheek and tug on her facial muscles. Call me a chicken, but I just couldn't stomach the thought of that being me.

Now I want to be clear that just because plastic surgery is not the right choice for *me*, I'm certainly not against it. Plastic surgery started as reconstructive surgery, and I wholeheartedly support that. My sister Cindi had to endure twenty-three such surgeries after a horrible accident when she was driving to the airport and someone dropped a vat of sulfuric acid from an overpass. It shattered her windshield and landed all over her, burning her face and body beyond recognition. Plastic surgery was the only answer for her, and I am so thankful that it helped give her back a lip, her nose, and part of her eyelids. Another example is my mother. Her breasts were so huge that she had to have special bras made. There were deep, red, raw indents in her shoulders from her bra, and her back ached all the time. At least once a day when I was growing up, she'd say, "I wish I could have these things reduced." Of course, that was the last thing we had money for, but today it breaks my heart that my precious, hardworking mother never got to alleviate her discomfort and excessive pain with a breast reduction.

I know those were two medical examples, but even if your goal for plastic surgery is purely cosmetic, I think that's okay as long as you're doing it for the right reasons. For example, if you have a good self-image but changing something you don't like about your body is going to make you feel better about life, then I believe that it's okay to go ahead and do it. But if you're getting plastic surgery because you think you are going to like yourself more as a result (or someone else will), I say step away from the doctor's office because even the prettiest face can't guarantee that and perhaps it's time to work on how you feel inside.

I firmly believe that you can look your best at any age without going under the knife. I'll also be honest and say that even with the best diet, exercise, and skin care regimen, your body naturally changes with each passing birthday and some of it is not pretty. Wrinkles happen. So does sagging. And this occurs in some places you'd never expect. For example, I assumed my face would age, but who knew that the skin on my arms would get crinkly, my elbows would wrinkle, or that I'd have sagging skin around my knees? Now, I can hate those arms, elbows, and knees and dwell on how bad they look or I can embrace each new year and do what I can to look my best. I choose to do the latter because a long time ago I accepted the fact that I'm not always going to look twenty or thirty—or even forty or fifty—forever. And truth be told, I don't want to.

Robin's Rx One reason skin sags is that the muscles beneath it get lax as we age. The best way to reduce this slacking skin is to tighten these muscles and certain facial exercises can strengthen them and give your face a lift. The other benefit to facial exercises is that they boost circulation to the skin, which gives you that youthful, rosy glow. Here are a few that Janet suggests doing to look younger—naturally!

Neck and Jaw Firming Exercise

You can do this exercise standing or sitting. However, you do have to tilt your head back, so if you have any issues with maintaining your balance you may want to choose a seated position.

- Stand or sit with your shoulders back, down, and relaxed and your spine straight.
- Hold your tongue against the roof of your mouth and slowly lift your chin upward. As you do so, you will start to feel the muscles on the front of your neck tighten. This is perfect and exactly what you want to feel.
- Once your muscles feel tightest, your head will be tilted back. Then hold that position and push your chin upward and out, almost like you're creating an under-bite. Do this 14 times and then rest for 30 seconds with your face forward and relaxed.
- Repeat this series of movements three times. For best results, do this in the morning and in the evening.

Midface and Cheek Exercise

This short exercise involves a facial stretch that will elevate your cheeks and reduce slacking skin in the midface.

- Sit facing forward with your shoulders square to the front and back and your chin up.
- Place your index finger on your chin gently (this will create some resistance).
- Open your mouth slowly and tighten your lips so they roll in over your teeth and start to tighten your entire middle face by lowering your jaw and tightening as you open slowly.

- Push down on your chin with your index finger and create a little resistance as you look upward and tilt your head back only slightly. Your mouth should be open, lips tight, and eyes upward, then relax.
- Once you feel the maximum amount of muscular tension in your face, hold the expression for 20 seconds, then release. Repeat this exercise eight times in the morning and eight times in the evening.

Reaching the age of fifty-five means that I have two grown sons and a wonderful daughter-in-law and have been married to a man I love and respect for more than three decades. I am at peace with the path I've chosen and role I've played in my husband's and children's lives. I am so proud of the amazing men that my two boys have grown into that when I'm with them, I *want* to look like their mother. Erica, my thirty-year-old daughter-in-law is absolutely beautiful (inside and out), and I love the youthful radiance she exudes. But I'm so honored to be her mother-in-law that when I'm with her I *want* the world to know that I am her mother-in-law—not wonder if I'm her sister. I love everything I've worked for and earned in these fifty-five years and, even if I could, I wouldn't erase one single, solitary year.

That doesn't mean that I don't want to look as good as I can for my age. Some people think those two notions—embracing your age and wanting to look your best—can't coexist, and I get plenty of letters and e-mails from people who question this. Yet to me aging gracefully isn't accepting what aging does to you. It means taking care of yourself, wanting to look your best, and knowing that it is not conceited, egotistical, or selfish to do so.

Many people ask me what I've done to keep my skin looking young and healthy. Oddly enough, the best thing I've done was also the most unintentional, and that was steering clear of the sun from the time I was a little girl. Growing up, I had very fair skin, red hair, and freckles—a combination that experts say makes you most susceptible to sunburn. Each summer, our big family vacation was to go visit my dad's mother, Granny Opal, in Norman, Oklahoma. She was a hostess at the restaurant at the Holiday Inn, so while she worked, my brother, sisters, and I got to spend the whole day at the hotel, splashing around in the pool and eating lunch outside, a treat that otherwise would have been unimaginable for a poor family like ours.

All that changed for me the first day of vacation when I was thirteen years old. After hours playing outside and in the pool, I got sunburned to a crisp. Blisters covered my face and body, and my skin was so scorched that even the gentlest touch felt like a slap. I spent the whole night writhing in pain while Granny Opal applied compresses drenched in ice-cold milk (milk protein is a natural anti-inflammatory, so it calms the skin and its fat content and acidic pH have a soothing, drying effect). The pain lasted for over a week as my skin cracked and the blisters turned to scabs. The rest of that trip—and all subsequent summer visits to Granny Opal—my four siblings played happily in the Holiday Inn pool while I spent the day reading a book under an umbrella wearing long sleeves and a hat.

From that day forward, I avoided the sun whenever possible. I was nineteen years old when I first started dating Phillip, and I remember how his mother and sisters would grease themselves up with baby oil and iodine, a combination that helps enhance a tan by attracting more sunlight. Then they'd lie on a blanket in the backyard and fry themselves in the hot Texas sun for hours. They'd invite me along, and though I did want to get to know Phillip's family, I'd remember my experience at the

Holiday Inn and politely decline their invitation. And you know what? When I talk to Phillip's mother and sisters about this today, they say that their sun-damaged skin makes them wish they'd stayed inside. Even when Jay and Jordan took up scuba diving and we'd vacation in sunny locales like the Cayman Islands, I stayed inside reading a book, which was something I enjoyed more. On occasion when I did sit outside, I was always in the shade, fully clothed, wearing a hat, sunscreen, and sunglasses. I did the same when I kept score for the boys' baseball teams, dragging my own little umbrella, lawn chair, and broad-brimmed hat to each game.

It seems almost amazing that the sun could have such a huge impact on how our skin ages, but it's true. Over the years, I've asked many, many dermatologists the same question: what's the best product to protect against aging? The unanimous answer? Sunscreen. The first few times I heard this I was surprised because I expected them to tell me about some ridiculously expensive product that was made with some hard-to-find ingredient. But I was convinced that they were right when I learned that only 20 percent of skin's aging is genetic, while 80 percent is the result of accumulated sun damage, which is called "photoaging.[1] That's because the sun's rays actually thin the skin and break down two of its important support structures: collagen and elastin. The bright side of that staggering statistic is that we can do a lot to ward off the wrinkles, dullness, and age spots that we dread by simply avoiding the sun as much as possible and wearing sunscreen every day, year round. And this is the case even if you never go to the beach or lie in the sun, because just the incidental exposure you get from things like walking to your car, mailbox, or office, sitting on the sidelines at your kids' soccer games, or driving (yes, research shows that the sun's rays can get through a closed car window) adds up and can cause damage.

Unfortunately, the dangers of the sun go beyond vanity. UV rays can cause skin cancer, a potentially deadly disease that more than one million Americans will be diagnosed with this year, according to the Skin Cancer Foundation.[2] This is more than all other types of cancer combined! I'm actually amazed that despite well-publicized reports about the incidence of this disease and how much the sun can age you, many women still lie out. I'm especially perplexed when I see photos of actresses basking in the sun because these women are in an industry where a few wrinkles can be the difference between getting a part and not getting one. Other women opt for tanning booths because they think they're safer, but recent research reveals that this is a myth. In fact, some of the newer sunlamps give off UV rays that are twelve times stronger than the real thing.[3] I wish I could tell that to one million Americans who go to tanning salons every day![4]

Robin's Rx Each month, I examine my skin from head to toe to make sure none of my brown spots or moles have changed or that no new ones have cropped up (both possible signs of skin cancer). I urge you to do the same on yourself (and your children if you have them) as well as have an annual professional skin exam. Though a dermatologist's office appointment may not be in your budget, the American Academy of Dermatology offers free skin cancer screenings nationwide. (Visit their Web site www.aad.org for more information).

Besides avoiding the sun, there are a few other things you can start early to ward off aging skin later in life. The first is making sure you get enough sleep and the second is avoiding alcohol and nicotine. Getting enough sleep was easy for me back in my early twenties because I worked during the day and went to school at night so there was little time (or money) to stay out late. Also, because both Phillip's father and my own were alcoholics and we knew that was something we did not want in our lives, we didn't spend nights out at smoke-filled bars. Again, I didn't do this to benefit my skin, but looking back I realize that it had a huge impact and sometimes I wish I could impress this upon the many young women I meet or the hard-partying twentysomething celebrities we can't help but hear about. I'm all for having fun and enjoying a glass of wine with good friends, but regularly staying out until the wee hours of the night in smoke-filled bars can affect your body and skin decades from now. I hear young women say that there's no harm in those late nights and they're going to do this now before they have children and settle down. That's fine once in a while, but what they don't realize is that the alcohol they're sipping and cigarettes they're puffing are wreaking havoc on their complexions.

Alcohol dehydrates your skin and can cause broken or distended capillaries on the nose and face. Smoking reduces the amount of oxygen and circulation to the skin so it looks dull and exposes it to damaging free radicals, particles that damage skin cells and break down collagen. In fact, one study found that wrinkles which may not be visible to the naked eye can be seen under a microscope in smokers as young as twenty years old.[5] Smoking also prevents skin from healing which only magnifies the negative impact of the sun, and even secondhand smoke can have this affect. Janet Harris, a renowned aesthetician, owner of the Skin Rejuvenation Center in Beverly Hills and creator of an array of skin-care products, has said that she can tell if a facial client is a smoker because of the nicotine smell and yellow gunk that seeps out of her pores. (Gross, isn't it?)

Plus, while the hours from 11:00 p.m. to 5:00 a.m. may be prime time for partying, they're also prime time for your skin to do some important work. "Skin cells naturally renew and repair themselves when you're in one of the deepest states of sleep," says Janet. "So if you're up most of the night, you're missing out on your skin's natural anti-aging treatment." The other thing about your skin at night is that the difference in its pH and its improved circulation makes it easier for active ingredients in products like wrinkle or acne creams to penetrate better. These ingredients also remain more potent since they're not exposed to things like sun, wind, or sweat like they are if you use them during the day.

What makes late nights out even more of a problem is if you come home too exhausted to do much but flop into bed and then you fall asleep with a face full of makeup (and smoke and other grime you've accumulated over the course of the day). Now, if I have one cardinal rule of skin care, it's to remove my makeup before going to bed. I often joke that you could hold a gun on me and I would not go to sleep without scrubbing my face. (But I'm not even sure if I'm joking.) From the minute I started wearing makeup in high school, my older sisters told me to remove every bit of it before bed and to this day I'm thankful for that advice. There were nights after studying or work when I could barely keep my eyes open but would force myself to wash up. (A few times I have fallen asleep on the sofa and still cleaned my face before I went to bed!)

Dermatologists and aestheticians I've queried about this have said the same things my sisters said way back when: the makeup—along with the day's worth of dirt and oil—can clog your pores, causing breakouts. Plus, dirty pores may actually stretch, making them appear more noticeable. "Makeup also suffocates your skin so it can't breathe," says Janet. "As a result, it's harder for it to renew itself while you sleep." Even eye makeup like mascara is a problem because it can dry out and cause breakage to your lashes. These delicate hairs naturally get sparser and lose their lushness as you age, so why speed up the process?

Now, despite my good intentions and the positive things I did for my complexion, I have still suffered from various skin problems over the years. In my twenties, I found out that I had a disease called folliculitis, which is an infection of the hair follicles. Some forms of this condition clear up on their own, but I still experience bouts of it today in a very small patch on my chin. Prescription medications have helped, but the best thing for me is tweezing the hair follicles to open them up. Thirty years later, experts like Janet have told me that I could probably remedy this with laser hair removal, but I actually find tweezing the hairs (only about twenty-five of them) to be relaxing.

By the time my thirties rolled around, I was stunned when I developed acne—a skin condition I thought I'd left back in my teenage years along with big hair and blue eye shadow. I thought for sure something was wrong with me, but after a visit to a dermatologist I learned that it's actually pretty common in women in their thirties and forties, and you can get it even if you never had it as a teen. Experts link it to hormonal changes that result from pregnancy, birth control pills, stress, perimenopause, and menopause. I also learned that my pores were slanted, making it harder for me to clean any dirt or oil out of them. This left them clogged and the result was a smattering of pimples on my cheeks, chin, and nose. My problem was that I loved to pick and squeeze and just couldn't keep my hands off of my face. I'd feel a blemish under the skin and, impatient for it to reach the surface, I'd start picking it. But this just made matters worse because not only did I have a pimple, I then had a dark spot on my skin that would take weeks or even months to disappear. I later learned that this is a common condition called postinflammatory hyperpigmentation, which results when skin becomes inflamed from a pimple (even one you don't pick) or injury and its pigment-making cells produce excess pigmentation in response.

My dermatologist tried to treat my adult acne with various oral antibiotics, which made me nauseated, and topical gels and lotions, which didn't work. Finally, he suggested I go on Accutane, a powerful oral medicine prescribed for moderate to severe acne that doesn't respond to other forms of treatment. Though I'm reluctant to take synthetic drugs and knew this one had a reputation for harsh side effects, I believed my doctor when he said my acne wasn't going to clear up on its own. Within three months, it was gone, and I've never had a problem with acne since. (Though I also attribute that to being on top of my hormones and keeping them in check, which we'll discuss in chapter 5.)

Even though I'd always cared for my skin, I stepped it up a notch after experiencing adult acne and hearing about the slanted state of my pores. That's when, at the suggestion of an older friend with flawless skin, I began getting facials. The first time I booked an appointment at the spa she went to, and after an hour of having my skin scrubbed, squeezed, and moisturized, I was hooked. Not only was it soothing for my face, but for my mind. As a busy mother of two who was always running and doing for everyone else, it was nice to slow down and get pampered. Even though we couldn't afford regular facials, it was something I'd save up for or ask for as a gift when holidays or my birthday rolled around. (Try it yourself: this makes life easy for the gift-giver and means you're not stuck with a present you don't like.) I learned a lot from the aestheticians who worked on my skin, and one of the best tips I got was to drink at least eight glasses of water a day. I immediately lost a few pounds, but I also noticed that my skin looked clearer and fresher than ever. "Hydrating skin—both from the inside and out—plumps it up, making it harder to see any fine lines and wrinkles," Janet explains. It can also give it a glow.

Robin's Rx I know one reason I get so many compliments on my skin is because I get facials by Yolanda, a Los Angeles-based private facialist. Here's a facial scrub she uses on me that I absolutely love: Combine four tablespoons of refined brown sugar, a tablespoon of olive oil, and mashed-up petals from half of a fresh red or pink rose. Apply to damp skin and scrub gently using circular motions for one to two minutes. Rinse with warm water, pat skin dry, and apply your favorite moisturizer.

I also started exfoliating with a homemade scrub I'd make by combining one cup of oatmeal, one cup of almonds, and half a cup of honey in a blender until smooth. (If you store it in the fridge, it can last over a week. It hardens and thickens a bit, so leave it out to soften before using it or add a little water to it in the palm of your hand.) Just like I still do today, I'd scrub it gently on my face for a minute and then remove it with a washcloth and cold water. Exfoliating, according to Janet and other skin experts and makeup artists whom I've talked to, is the most important thing that women age thirty and up can do for their skin. That's because our topmost layer of skin is constantly dying and sloughing itself off to reveal newer, fresher skin cells. However, as you get older your skin's ability to remove these cells slows, which is why skin tends to look duller and less radiant than it used to. Exfoliating speeds this process up so you get that youthful glow and it makes it easier for your treatment products like wrinkle and acne fighters to penetrate the skin since there's no dead layer of cells for them to get through. It also creates a smoother surface on which to apply your makeup so it looks more natural.

By my forties, I'd been taking really good care of my skin, was taking dietary supplements, and was in control of my hormones, so my skin actually looked pretty good. The only thing I noticed was enlarged pores—as if their being slanted wasn't enough! This is actually common as you age because when collagen breaks down, skin becomes looser and stretches slightly. This, along with gravity, can make pores look bigger. Plus, since your complexion isn't as plump, the skin around the pores doesn't conceal them as much. I had heard that something called a FotoFacial helped decrease pore size and improve skin texture, so I tried one. In these noninvasive thirty- to forty-five-minute treatments, a doctor or aesthetician uses a handheld instrument (it looks sort of like a wand) to zap the skin with intense pulsed light, which is said to be much gentler than laser light. Lasers can also require a few days of downtime, whereas with the FotoFacial I could go in and emerge for 3:00 p.m.

car pool looking totally normal. After a series of six such treatments, my pores were less obvious and my skin seemed smoother.

Despite that positive spa experience, here's a cautionary tale. Several months after the FotoFacials, the spa director (whom I'll call Sally) called to tell me she had a new machine she was just dying to try. "It's perfect for your skin," she gushed. Though it's very uncharacteristic of me, I made an appointment without asking any questions. I didn't know the name of the machine, what it did, and why it was so perfect for me. For some reason I got swept up in Sally's excitement and trusted that this was a good thing—a mistake I'd never make again. Before the treatment, Sally told me that it would be very relaxing and painless. *Great,* I thought, as I slipped on my headphones and closed my eyes. But the first time she applied the handheld device to my skin, I felt a hot, stabbing sensation. *Maybe that's just the initial shock,* I thought. That was until it happened again and again and again. Finally, I stopped her. "Sally, this really hurts," I said. "It feels like you're burning me."

"Really? It's not supposed to hurt," she said. "Let me go call the manufacturer."

She disappeared into the next room and when she came back minutes later all the color had drained out of her face. "Robin, I am so sorry," she said, practically in tears. "By mistake, I used the highest setting on the machine when I should have been using the lowest!"

By that point my neck and chest were bright red and throbbing and all I wanted was to get home. Over the course of the next few days the skin started coming off in raw, painful sheets and then turned blackish-purple as scabs formed. I am not sure what was worse: the pain or the fear that my skin was scarred or damaged forever. *Smooth skin is not worth all this,* I thought. To add a not-so-funny twist, Jay's first book had recently come out, and the TV show *Entertainment Tonight* called asking if they could interview me about being the mother of a *New York Times* best-selling author.

Just a few days earlier, I winced anytime anything touched my skin, but luckily by the interview the pain had subsided enough to slip on a very high turtleneck (a good thing because I can just imagine the rumors that would have started if they'd gotten a glimpse of my burnt and battered décolletage). The moral of that painful story is this: be an informed consumer no matter what you're going to try. Ask questions and ask a lot of them. Find out what a treatment does, why the doctor or aesthetician thinks you need it, and how many similar treatments he or she has done so far. Then, don't just take his or her word for it, but go home and do your own research by looking at the manufacturer's Web site, getting a second opinion, and talking to other women who've had the procedure done.

A few years after that fiasco, we moved to California for Phillip's show. That's when I discovered the treatment I credit for my youthful complexion and one reason I think people assume I've had a face-lift. I had been living in Los Angeles for just a few months and went to a local spa for a facial. There, the aesthetician suggested I try a Medi-Lift, a forty-five-minute treatment she said she did on women from their twenties to their seventies. After extensive research, I made an appointment. The treatment entails having little, pulsating electrodes placed all over your face for forty-five minutes. In that time, they're working the muscles of your face to what's said to be the equivalent to five hours in a gym so that skin is less saggy and more toned. I did the required series of six treatments over the course of about three weeks and have been going for monthly maintenance sessions ever since. (Compared to many treatments it isn't too pricey, about $150–$300 per treatment depending on where you are in the country.)

That was six years ago, and I swear this and my history of hiding in the shade are what keep my skin in top shape. Of course, genetics has played a role, too, because the other things that have kept my skin from wrinkling are my naturally high levels of human growth hormone and testosterone (but more on that in chapter 5) and just staying on top of my hormones in general. This helped so much that even through menopause I didn't suffer from the dryness or breakouts that are common.

In addition to the monthly Medi-Lift and monthly facials, my daily regimen is actually quite simple. In the morning, I wake up and wash my face with Purpose Cleansing Wash, a gentle oil- and soap-free cleanser, or Janet's Skin Care Daily Phacial Wash, which contains glycolic acid and aloe vera. I know many people don't wash their face in the morning, but my skin can get oily at night and if I use a treatment product—like a blemish cream or wrinkle treatment—it can leave a residue that needs to be washed off.

After cleansing my face, I splash it with the coldest water I can stand (a trick my mother and sisters taught me as a teen) to help close the pores and give my skin a glow. Next, I pat my face dry with a soft towel and apply Janet's Skin Care Kine-phirm Serum, and Janet's Skin Care Moisture-Phase Repair Cream with Kine-phirm, both of which contain kine-phirm, aloe vera, and vitamins C and E, to the still-damp skin on my face, neck, and chest, which helps seal in moisture. Once that is completely dry, I apply Janet's Skin Care Sunscreen Moisturizer, which contains an SPF 15 and the sunblock titanium dioxide, and then my makeup. On my body, I use a homemade scrub in the shower (it combines a half cup each of brown sugar, white sugar, coarse salt, and chopped cranberries with two tablespoons of essential oil) and after I dry off, I slather on Frederick Fekkai Shea Butter, a cream that softens skin with natural shea butter and almond protein. Or if I need extra hydration, I combine a body lotion with one of my favorite essential oils like lavender, blend it together in my hands, and use that.

After a day of taping two or three shows, I have a face full of heavy makeup, which I scrub off as soon as I get home. First, I place a very warm washcloth on my face in order to start melting off all that makeup—especially mascara. I follow this with one of my gentle cleansers (and wash my face more than once to really make sure I've removed everything) and then I use my home-made oatmeal-honey-almond scrub. My final step: covering my face with Dr. Eckstein's Azulene Paste, a calming cream that comes from the azulene plant. The word *paste* sounds awful and brings to mind images of preschool art projects, not skin care, but I swear by it. I spread it on my skin like a mask, and it nourishes my complexion, leaving it smooth and dewy after a long day in heavy makeup. (I don't rinse it off; rather, it absorbs into the skin.) I also dab it on when I have a blemish and it clears it up quickly.

Then I go about the rest of my day, and before bed I simply apply Janet's Skin Care Moisture-Phase Repair Cream with Kine-phirm, Jack Black Intense Therapy Lip Balm, which contains shea butter, avocado oil, vitamin E, green tea and the sunblock Avobenzone and, if needed, a treatment product like LCP Vitamin C Infusion Cream, which contains a high concentration and stable form of vitamin C so it actually penetrates skin. Then, I call it a day and focus on the most important part of my skin-care regimen: getting at least eight hours of sleep. Of course, if I've had to reapply makeup to go out in the evening, then I repeat my facial cleansing and makeup-removing regimen.

Robin's Rx Janet shared this fabulous nighttime moisturizing treatment with me, and I think it's just terrific. Combine half a teaspoon of evening primrose oil with two drops of neroli oil (both available at health food stores). The hydrating properties of these oils help pamper dry skin, while the aromatherapeutic effects help you calm down and relax.

Before I end here, I want to mention two more important points about skin care and beauty. Though I'm all for using inexpensive products (and today there are so many wonderful options) or even the homemade variety,

I also believe that if a product, procedure, or treatment is going to truly change your life, then it may be worth investing in it. I've heard women say that their lives and self-esteem were transformed by whitening the yellow teeth they'd been hiding for decades. Or that after finally seeking professional treatment to clear up their acne, they had confidence for the first time in their lives. This happened to one of my sisters.

One day about twenty years ago, my sister and I were talking on the phone when she expressed frustration over her facial hair. Her problem wasn't just a wiry strand here or a mustache there, but a full-on beard that she had to shave every day—sometimes twice. (She'd even get up before her husband to shave it so he wouldn't notice it.) We'd talked about this problem many, many times before, but that day I realized it was taking over her life and affecting her self-esteem. Tearfully, she talked about how embarrassed she was to leave the house or see anyone she knew. We didn't have a lot of money back then, but at that moment I decided that I would save up and help her pay for electrolysis, a procedure in which an electrical current permanently destroys the hair follicle. When I told her this she broke down with tears of joy. After ten sessions, the hair was gone. It changed not only how she looked, but more importantly how she felt about herself and her outlook on life. And to me, well, that's priceless.

The other thing about skin care and beauty is that they are more than something to pamper your skin. They can pamper your mind. Many viewers write in telling me how they've let themselves go, and to them and you I say, go find yourself again. Even though you're a wife and mother, you're still a woman. You should take time for yourself, and even a simple treatment—whether it's rubbing foot cream on your soles, taking a bath, or splurging at the spa—can do wonders for your spirit as well as your looks. Life is hard, which is all the more reason you need to treat yourself. You'd be amazed at how much doing a face mask (available at the drugstore for just a few dollars or simply spread on a whipped egg white) can mentally rejuvenate you. It also sends a message to your family and, more importantly, to yourself that you *are* worth being cared for.

Though what provides us with a sense of serenity varies from woman to woman, my peace of mind has always depended on a long soak in the tub. And I can remember exactly when that started. Jay was just three weeks old, and I was still in that new mom haze where taking a shower seemed like an impossible feat. That night when Phillip came home, I handed him the baby and got in the shower. I hadn't even finished sudsing my hair when I saw Phillip holding Jay over the top of the shower door. Jay's face was bright red (though still adorable), and he was wailing at the top of his tiny lungs.

"Phillip, what are you doing?" I asked.

"He was crying, and I thought if he saw you he'd stop."

Robin's Rx When we were pregnant, my grandmother told my three sisters and me to buy Bag Balm, a lanolin-rich product that has been used as a salve on cow udders since 1899 and is found at the feed and grain store. She told us to slather it on our pregnant bellies to ward off stretch marks, and though it may be a coincidence, not one of us had them. Now this product is far from elegant—it's thick, sticky, and smells like rubber. But it worked back then, and to this day I use it when my heels, elbows, or lips are super dry.

"Please take that baby out of here right now and let me finish my shower," I said. As I finished washing up, I decided then and there that I needed to set boundaries and let my family know that I was still going to be a woman even though I was a mother and a wife. From that day forward, I made at least half an hour after dinner a time for me and me alone. Phillip would come home from work, and I'd hand over the boys and head to the bathroom. As the boys got older, they understood that when Mom goes into the bathroom it's her time and that, unless someone is bleeding, they should direct all questions and concerns to their father.

Even though the kids are grown, I still do this. Sometimes I'll put on a facial mask, light a candle, and play music. Other times I just dim the lights and climb in the tub. As I sit there, I mull over a problem, plan my week, or just zone out and think about nothing. At the end of my bath, I often say a prayer thanking the Lord for all he has blessed me with. I ask him for his help and guidance with my life and the lives I touch. Sometimes I focus on one person or many, be it loved ones or strangers. Of course, I always ask that he bless and protect my husband and children.

For the price of an unhealthy candy bar or trashy tabloid, you could buy some bubble bath or a lovely candle and find your own little piece of Zen. But more than that, you can show the world and yourself that you are more than a mother and a wife. Phillip always says that we teach people how to treat us. Teach your family, friends, and yourself that you are a woman who deserves loving care and attention.

Answers from the Expert

Janet Harris, a renowned aesthetician, owner of the Skin Rejuvenation Center in Beverly Hills and creator of an array of skin care products.

If I can only afford one treatment, what's the best thing I can do for my skin?

There's no one treatment short of surgery that will erase the years. Instead of spending a lot of money on one treatment at a dermatologist's office or spa, you're better off buying a product you can use daily, because it's the maintenance of your skin over the long term that can improve it.

I'm confused by all the anti-aging hype. What really works on lines and wrinkles?

Wrinkles occur as we age because the skin's support structures, collagen, and elastin, break down thanks to the natural aging process, sun damage, and repetitive movements like smiling, squinting, eating, talking, kissing, smoking, and frowning. (Amazingly, people in their eighties have four times more broken collagen than those in their twenties.[6]) Research shows that over 80 percent of women say that the first place they see signs of aging is around their eyes. This makes sense, because the skin in that area is thinner than elsewhere on the body and thus breaks down more easily. Also, most of us don't put sunscreen around the eyes because it can be irritating, so this thin skin can get a lot of sun damage. (Avoid this by looking for eye creams that contain sunscreen since they're gentler than sunscreens made for the rest of the body.)

Also, skin becomes an estimated 10 percent drier each decade due to a decrease in estrogen, oil glands, and its ability to contain moisture. Unfortunately, dry skin makes wrinkles more noticeable and will break down more rapidly. That means it's key to hydrate skin, both with a good moisturizer and by drinking water, since this can temporarily plump skin so wrinkles aren't as noticeable. It's best to apply your lotion or cream to damp—not totally dry—skin to help seal moisture in. (This goes for your face or body).

The best way to prevent or smooth wrinkles is with products that contain ingredients that stimulate the growth of new collagen and those that protect skin from further damage. These ingredients include the following:

- Retinoic acid is a form of vitamin A (also called retinol in over-the-counter products or Retina-A in higher-strength prescription products). Most doctors agree that this is the workhorse of the wrinkle smoothers because it has so much research—about thirty years' worth—to show that it helps stimulate collagen and speeds cell turnover. Most forms of retinoic acid make skin more sun sensitive, so be diligent about sunscreen and stop using them for two weeks before any treatment like waxing or laser hair removal. If you opt for the prescription product, do so while being monitored by a doctor, use it for just four to twelve weeks since it can thin skin, and avoid it if you're pregnant or nursing.

- Hyaluronic acid is something that our bodies naturally produce to keep skin firm (it's also in our joints), but the amount diminishes as we age. It's believed to both rejuvenate skin so it helps with wrinkles, and it attracts moisture from the air to keep skin hydrated.

- Peptides are a group of amino acids that are believed to help the skin produce collagen and inhibit the enzymes that break down the skin's support structures so they prevent future wrinkles.

- Antioxidants help fight wrinkles by protecting the skin from free radical damage and some are believed to help boost collagen production. Apply them topically by using products that contain green tea, white tea, vitamin C, to name just a few, and take them internally by sipping green tea and eating a lot of fruits and veggies.

- Glycolic and salicylic acids are often found in at-home peel kits. They work by exfoliating the top layer of skin, which can smooth very fine wrinkles.

One caveat: Most of these ingredients can do a lot for fine lines and wrinkles, but for really deep grooves, you'll likely have to have doctor's office or spa treatments for best results.

I'm in my twenties. What should I be doing today to look better tomorrow?

It's never too early to start caring for your skin. Amazingly, by the time you're in your teens or twenties, you've already been exposed to environmental damage and *preventing* wrinkles, brown spots, and other damage is a lot easier than fixing it.

If you follow these three rules, you'll look gorgeous with each passing birthday: *exfoliate*, *hydrate*, and *protect*. Exfoliate skin to remove dead cells and give skin a glow; hydrate by using a good moisturizer and drinking around eight 8-ounce glasses of water daily; protect against damage with sunscreen (don't forget your hands since they're one of the first places to show signs of aging) and antioxidants, both topically and by eating a healthy diet.

My skin care products don't seem to be working. Is it because they're inexpensive rather than from some pricey line?

No. There are many very effective active ingredients, like retinol, peptides, or vitamin C, to name just a few, that are easy to find in inexpensive skin-care lines. Additionally, many of the companies that manufacture inexpensive skin-care products—like Neutrogena, Aveeno, and Dove—have the money and resources to extensively research their products to make sure they're effective. Perhaps your products don't seem to be working because you're not giving them enough time—at least three to four months—to do their job. In our fast-paced world, we all want results yesterday, but skin doesn't work like that. After all, it takes thirty days for a skin cell to turn over, so you have to be patient and give products time to affect the surface layer of the skin.

What's the best way to banish breakouts?

Several ingredients help clear up pimples and prevent new ones. Salicylic acid is an antibacterial ingredient that removes the potentially pore-clogging top layer of dead cells and helps remove dirt and oil. Look for over-the-counter products, like cleansers and treatment products, that contain 2 percent salicylic acid, but use 1 percent if skin is sensitive. Another pimple fighter is benzoyl peroxide, which unclogs pores and kills bacteria. However, it can be irritating and drying, so avoid it if skin is dry or sensitive. If at-home acne products don't work after a few weeks, see a dermatologist who can prescribe stronger medications or recommend treatments like laser or light therapy.

How you care for your skin can affect pimples or acne. Many people think breakouts mean that skin is dirty, so they overscrub and overcleanse. This is a bad idea since it irritates your already-irritated complexion and dehydrates skin, causing it to produce excess oil, which just causes more breakouts. Also, if you wear makeup, make sure products say "noncomedogenic" on the label, which means that they won't clog pores, or look for mineral makeup, which tends to be gentle on your complexion.

What can I do about cellulite?

You're certainly not alone in your quest to get rid of these not-so-adorable dimples. It's estimated that more than 85 percent of women have cellulite, which is why if there were truly a cure, you'd know about it. However, there are a few things you can do to reduce its appearance. The best is to exercise and lose weight—excess fat below the surface of the skin can make it more noticeable. Though no cream is a miracle cure, those with caffeine green tea, ginkgo biloba, menthol, or camphor may work temporarily by increasing circulation to the area and increasing lymphatic drainage. For best results, you may want to invest in a spa treatment that uses VelaShape, the only machine that is FDA-approved to treat cellulite. It's said to work by helping the body burn fat and by increasing circulation to the dimple-ridden area. Again, it's not a magic bullet, but it can help.

As I've gotten older, my skin has lots of brown spots and discolorations. Any tips?

Most dark spots and discolorations result when sun damage from your past makes its way to the surface. Exfoliating can help remove the dead cells, taking some of the pigment with it. You can use physical exfoliators, like scrubs with small particles, facial puffs, or at-home microdermabrasion kits or chemical exfoliators, like over-the-counter peel products or lotions that contain glycolic, salicylic, or lactic acid, to name just a few. You can also fade spots with hydroquinone, the strongest over-the-counter lightening ingredient which works by turning off the skin's pigment producing enzymes. Wearing sunscreen of at least SPF 30 every day will significantly lighten dark spots—and prevent new ones—because they're not getting stimulated to make more pigment. If at-home treatments like these don't work, see a dermatologist or expert at a medical spa.

Do you have any tips for trying new products?

- Do a patch test by applying a small amount to an area of skin like that behind the ear or on the upper inner thigh and wait twenty-four hours to see if you experience any redness, irritation, or burning.
- Follow the instructions, and use only the amount they suggest. Sometimes we think more is better, but it could increase the risk of side effects.
- Don't combine one product with certain active ingredients with another with the same active ingredients—it could alter its efficacy and cause irritation.

What kind of sunscreen should I get?

The best sunscreens are those that block both ultraviolet B rays (UVB), which burn skin, and ultraviolet A rays (UVA), which penetrate deeper and cause signs of aging like sagging wrinkles, brown spots, and loss of elasticity. Look for the words "broad spectrum" or "UVA/UVB protection" on the label or ingredients that offer this protection like titanium dioxide, zinc oxide, avobenzone (also called Parsol 1789) and encamsule (also called Mexoryl). Choose one with the highest possible SPF. In addition to sunscreen, stay out of the sun and in the shade when the sun's rays are strongest (usually between 10:00 a.m. and 4:00 p.m.) and wear sunglasses (make sure lenses block 99 to 100 percent of UV rays) and a hat with at least a two-and-a-half-inch brim.

How do I know if a spot on my body is just an age spot or skin cancer?

It's not always easy to tell, so when in doubt make an appointment with a dermatologist. But here are some skin cancer warning signs, courtesy of the Skin Cancer Foundation:

- A spot or sore that constantly itches, hurts, crusts, bleeds, or scabs.
- An open sore that doesn't heal after two weeks' time.
- A skin growth, mole, beauty mark, or brown spot that changes texture, color, or size, is asymmetrical, has an irregular outline or border, is larger than the size of a pencil eraser and appears after the age of twenty-one or is pearly, translucent, tan, or multicolored.[7]

5

What's Hormones Got to Do with It?

The doctor handed me a thick stack of prescriptions. "Fill these and start taking them immediately," she said, pressing the small squares of paper into my hand. To say that I was perplexed is an understatement. I'd been in her office just a few minutes and, besides some brief pleasantries, that was the first thing she had said to me.

One week earlier, I'd come to see this new doctor (whom I'll call Dr. Gold) because I just hadn't felt like myself. I was experiencing occasional heart palpitations followed by a feeling of heat radiating throughout my body. On top of these physical symptoms, my mood was melancholy. Though I knew I was emotional because Jay was graduating from high school, I found myself spending too much time sitting around reflecting on his life and feeling sad.

None of these symptoms was particularly intense or overwhelming, and they certainly weren't debilitating. But as someone who knows her body, I could tell something wasn't right. I mentioned it to my sister Cindi, who thought it was probably my thyroid and suggested I get it checked. My gynecologist had recently retired, so at the recommendation of a friend, I made an appointment with Dr. Gold. When I went in and told her my symptoms and that I thought it was my thyroid, she nodded in agreement, asked very few questions, and took some blood.

Days later, I returned for the test results and that's when I got my stack of prescriptions. "Life as you know it is over," she said, shaking her head.

"What are all these?" I asked. "And how do you know that they're right for *me*?" Though she refrained from rolling her eyes, Dr. Gold's tone said it all: "Robin, you're in menopause. This is just what you have to do." I was almost waiting for her to say, "Now, run along." I was infuriated.

She was heading toward the door but stopped before she opened it. "I put an antidepressant in there, too, because your moods are *really* going to change," she said. "Trust me, you'll thank me later." Trust was about the last emotion I felt toward this woman who was sending me off into the night with the same prescriptions she'd likely give to any perimenopausal or menopausal woman who entered her office. To make matters worse, she didn't take any time, not even an extra minute, to explain the medications or to ask if I had any questions. I truly believe that one of our gifts as women is our intuition. It's usually dead-on, so if your gut makes you question something, listen to it. I didn't know much about perimenopause or menopause and admittedly felt a bit overwhelmed, but something told me that Dr. Gold's one-size-fits-all remedy wasn't right for me.

I left her office and got in my car, mulling over what I'd just experienced as I drove to Jordan's baseball game. There, I sat with Cora, another mom and good friend who was also a doctor. "Can you take a look at these and tell me what they are?" I asked her, pulling the prescriptions out of my purse. Besides the barely legible handwriting, I couldn't decipher the names of the medications.

"What's all this for?" Cora asked.

"My doctor said I'm in menopause."

"They're all synthetic medications. Is that what you want to do?" At that point, the phrase "synthetic medications" was foreign to me, so I shrugged my shoulders and asked, "Is it?"

"Well, expect a lot of changes in your body."

After the game, I couldn't get home fast enough. I pulled out those prescriptions, fired up my computer, and started researching not only the medications I was given, but the whole subject of menopause. Like the night my sister urged me to lose weight when it was five pounds not fifty, or the day my mother died, that moment was a pivotal one in my life. I realized even more so how important it was to take charge of my health and that if I didn't do it, no one else would. I also realized that I couldn't let any one-size-fits-all doctor tell me what to do (fill an armload of prescriptions) or how to feel (that life as I knew it was over). That was the start of my crusade to thoroughly research what I was putting in my body and the beginning of my very intense drive to educate myself about synthetic drugs and their natural alternatives. Prior to menopause, I didn't question the impact of synthetic medications because anything I took was short term, like antibiotics or Accutane. But now that my body was changing and I needed to help ease it through this transition, I had to become educated.

Ever since my mother died, I began taking care of myself as if my life depended on it because I couldn't stand the thought of my sons growing up without a mother or Phillip growing old without a wife. But that day in the doctor's office, I realized that I not only have to watch my health, but I have to work hard to make myself feel as good as I can. Often, when I hear women talk about menopause it's as if they're just bearing with it the way you do turbulence on an airplane by closing your eyes, holding your breath, and squeezing the armrests until it passes. The problem? The potential turbulence from perimenopause and menopause can affect months and years of your life—not mere minutes—and it's unlikely that avoiding it is going to make you feel better. In fact, it's just going to make you feel worse. For me, living with hot flashes, mood swings, night sweats, or any other symptoms of this life transition was unacceptable. I was not willing simply to muddle through menopause. I wanted to go through it feeling strong and powerful.

Though my symptoms weren't severe or debilitating like they are for many, many women, they *were* having an impact. Hot flashes, which 65 to 75 percent of perimenopausal and menopausal women experience,[1] were the most bothersome of my symptoms. I remember one particular day when I was hosting a hospital benefit luncheon at my house. There I was chatting with some lovely women I'd just met and pouring mimosas when all of a sudden I felt my heart beating rapidly in my chest and heat radiating throughout my body. After that, I broke out in a huge sweat and had perspiration dripping off my neck and lip. I didn't like the feeling that my body was controlling me (rather than the other way around), so I decided to become an expert in my menopause, how it was affecting my body, and how to make myself feel better. In addition to my online research, I'd go to the bookstore and plant myself in the health section. There, I'd flip through piles and piles of books on menopause and buy the ones that were of interest. Then every night, with Phillip watching TV in the chair beside me and Jay and Jordan doing their homework, I'd study those books.

From all my research, I learned the difference between perimenopause and menopause—a distinction that I'd never made before. Perimenopause is a period of time when your body starts its transition into menopause. Experts say how long it lasts varies from one woman to the next, but the range is two to eight years. Though it usually starts in your forties, some women go through it in their mid- to late thirties. During this time your body's levels of the hormones estrogen and progesterone rise and fall, and your periods change in some way, either getting longer or shorter, heavier or lighter, or farther apart. Menopause, on the other hand, begins one year after your periods stop altogether. Both perimenopause and menopause have an endless array of difficult and disruptive symptoms—such as weight gain, insomnia, acne, depression, low libido, forgetfulness, sore breasts, mood swings, anxiety, facial hair, bloating, and vaginal dryness, to name just a few—and various ways to treat them.

To me, the most appealing option was bio-identical hormones. The precursors to these hormones are derived primarily from plants, like soy or yam, and then converted into human hormones. "Bio-identical is a shortened term referring to 'human biologically identical hormones,' which means that they're exactly the same as the hormones Mother Nature put in our bodies to begin with," explains Jim Hrncir, RPh, of Las Colinas Pharmacy Compounding and Wellness Center in Irving, Texas. "Studies suggest that these hormones—if balanced correctly—have the greatest potential for minimizing health risks and improving a woman's quality of life. But it's important to note that over-the-counter supplements claiming to be bio-identical hormones are actually—according to the FDA—illegal, therefore the most appropriate treatment is to see a doctor to get prescription formulations so that your hormones are balanced and monitored."

On the other hand, many synthetic hormones aren't natural to the human body, so it can take days or weeks to break down each dose. "Because these substances are foreign to our bodies, there may be unnecessary and unpleasant side effects and an increase in risk factors," Jim explains. According to a study by the National Institutes of Health, the dangers of synthetic or unnatural hormone replacement therapy include increased risk of heart disease, stroke, and breast cancer. These potential risks were a huge concern of mine since my mother died of heart disease and my father died of cancer (albeit lung not breast cancer).

Now, before I continue and explain the path I took in handling my menopause, I want to make it clear that I *do* know that there are many respected doctors out there who disagree with my views on synthetic hormones and believe that, when taken under the care of a qualified physician, they have their benefits. What I'm going to describe is what I believe in and what worked for *me*. I am not a doctor, and I am not telling you what to do, but instead I am telling what I did during this time in my life. I don't consider myself an expert in biochemistry and bioscience, but I am an expert in my own body and consider myself to be a very informed woman. What follows is the plan that helped my body and that I believe made my transition into and through menopause a seamless one. I know this isn't the only path to take, but it's one that worked so well for me that I feel strongly about sharing it with you. That said, it's important to discuss any information and your own personal symptoms with a doctor or qualified health care provider before taking any medications or supplements (whether they're natural or otherwise).

After reading about bio-identical versus synthetic hormones, I was eager to find a doctor whose treatment entailed the former. Since these natural hormones need to be compounded, which means that they're specially customized and mixed upon the direction of a licensed physician, I decided to talk to the compounding pharmacists in my Dallas neighborhood (which is how I met Jim Hrncir). I asked them which doctors prescribe natural hormones and which doctors' patients seemed to return to time and time again. (To find a compounding pharmacist in your area, visit the Web site of the International Academy of Compounding Pharmacists at iacprx.org). I got recommendations for three doctors, made appointments with each of them, and found the one I liked best.

On a side note: I know that not everyone has the time or money to visit an array of doctors (only some of my appointments were covered by insurance), but even visiting just one doctor is a place to start. Also, this is your health we're talking about, so here's my advice. First, investigate what your insurance *does* cover. Then, if you still need to pay out-of-pocket for the kind of care you want, if you can do it, I suggest giving up whatever you need to afford it—whether that's a weekly dinner out, new shoes, or costly birthday parties for your kids—because nothing is more important than your health. Also, although pharmacists are certainly no replacement for a doctor, their extensive training can make them a valuable part of your health care team. In the past, I've called up Jim and other pharmacists and said, "Can I make an appointment to come and meet with you?" Then I've brought along the results of my blood work, told them what the doctor suggested, and asked their opinion. (Did I mention that I like to do a lot of research?) A pharmacist can also be helpful if you have to wait a few weeks for a doctor's appointment and simply want a suggestion for a supplement that can provide short-term relief to a bothersome symptom while you wait.

At the recommendation of one of the pharmacists, I started seeing a homeopathic practitioner who helped my hot flashes with acupuncture and a homeopathic remedy called sepia. Though you can get sepia at a health food store like Whole Foods, you can often get a more potent version from a homeopathic practitioner. (FYI: the key with any homeopathic remedy is that you shake it from the container to right under your tongue and never touch it with your hands.) Still, though I wanted to get rid of the hot flashes, I also needed to find out *why* I was having them in the first place, which is where one of the doctors who prescribed natural hormones came in. He took blood and had the lab evaluate all the hormones that are commonly affected during perimenopause and menopause, which include the various estrogens, progesterone, testosterone, DHEA, and pregnenolone. (If you're still getting your period, the best day to have your blood drawn, says Jim, is on day nineteen to twenty of your cycle, since that's when the progesterone and estrogen are highest.)

In addition, because menopause is a common time for the thyroid gland to be depleted, my doctor had the lab evaluate my free T3, which is the active thyroid hormone, free T4, which is the storage thyroid hormone, and thyroid stimulating hormone (TSH), which is what the pituitary gland uses to tell the body how much thyroid hormone you need. My blood work revealed that I was not producing enough estrogen or progesterone and that my thyroid was low. He prescribed the appropriate natural hormones. I remember being shocked that it's progesterone, not estrogen, that eases hot flashes. It wasn't until I found that out that I went on progesterone and my hot flashes were gone. He also prescribed supplements. Though all of this required a little tweaking here and there, within a short time I felt like my old self again. Actually, I felt better. Not only were my hot flashes and mood swings gone, but I had more stamina than I'd had in years, slept like a rock, and felt vibrant and energetic.

The other thing that really helped my transition through menopause was that I made it a family affair. Growing up, I remember my mother appearing flushed, sweaty, and irritable and saying, "Don't come in here!" as she retired to her bedroom for long stretches of the day. I realize now that she was suffering from menopause, but as a child I had no clue what was going on and really worried about her. As a result, I was determined that my boys, who were eleven and seventeen at the time, would never worry about me and that there would be no cloud of secrecy about my own journey through menopause. I knew that if I wanted my family to have a positive attitude about menopause, I had to have one too. I feel this is especially important if you have daughters who will one day experience perimenopause and menopause themselves. After all, you don't want them to dread a very natural experience in their future.

To help my own family, I sat my kids down and said, "Boys, here's the deal. I'm going through menopause, which means that my body's reacting in certain ways and so I may be different at times. This is not a bad thing. In fact, it's a very normal process in a woman's life, but there are certain things that are going to change around here." As I paused, Jay and Jordan squirmed a bit, unsure of what I was about to say. "One of them is that I'm going to be sleeping naked because I'm suffering from night sweats. That means that you can't just walk into our bedroom at night to tell us that you're home or that you're going to bed. You have to tap on the door and wait until your daddy or I tell you to come in." Though they looked at me like I'd given them a little too much information, I knew they got it. (And it *really* would have been too much information if they'd walked in on me in my birthday suit without warning!) Later that day, Jordan handed me a prized possession that he'd recently won at Six Flags: a little squirt bottle that had a fan attached to the nozzle. "Here, Mom," he said. "This will help cool you off." (Now if there's anything to make a hormonal mom cry, it's sweetness like that!)

My kids weren't the only ones I cautioned. I also gave America's Therapist a little heads-up. "You know Jay is leaving for college and at the same time I'm experiencing all these hormonal changes, which may make me a little on edge and irritable at times," I told Phillip. "So I'm going to need you to work with me and be a little patient."

"Okay, okay," he said nodding.

"But let me tell you something else," I added. "This does not give you free rein to blame every bad mood of mine or yours on the fact that I'm going through menopause." Again, he nodded in agreement.

I don't know what gave me the foresight to do this, but it was really helpful. The truth is, a lot of men are confused by women's emotional sides to begin with, so imagine how confused they are when the wife they've known for years is suddenly crying at the drop of a hat, angry for no apparent reason, or stripping naked at night (though I'm sure they'll let that last one slide). You have to be open and honest about what you're experiencing and get your family on board and explain what you're going through. After all, if you're unnerved by these changes, just think about how they'll feel. I remember a show where Phillip was counseling a bewildered husband whose wife was going through a really tough battle with menopause. Phillip told him, "You have to understand that this is an absolute, positive biological reality for your wife and that she didn't just wake up one day and decide to try getting away with raising hell every once in a while." Amen!

Robin's Rx Work with your doctor rather than passively sitting back and letting him or her be the only authority in the room. Your doctor is the health expert, and you are the expert on your body; the two of you can come together to find the answers that will make you feel the best that you can. I do enough research on how I'm feeling that when I go to see a doctor, it's almost like I know what he or she should be talking to me about. I don't want to say I know as much as a doctor because I certainly don't, and I look to them for their guidance and expertise. (And you *do* have to be wary of all the health misinformation that appears on the Internet.) But I at least make sure that I have a sense of what a doctor should be asking me about and what tests he or she will suggest.

Phillip used to say that he was really glad that I gave him forewarning that I was going through menopause; otherwise, during of some of my moodier moments, he would have been thinking, *Who are you and what have you done with my wife?* He was actually quite cute about it. I remember a few times when

I'd be a little on edge or moody and he'd say, "I don't want to get in trouble, so can I just ask you if you're having a hormonal moment or did I mess up and do something wrong?" If the answer was yes and I was having a hormonal moment, his saying this always lightened my mood and made me laugh.

I also garnered Phillip's support by keeping him informed about what I was experiencing and learning. I'd be reading one of my books and would stop and say, "Phillip, listen to what's happening to my body" or "Listen to what I have to do." He was very interested and understanding, and if he tired of my interrupting him while he watched his ball games, he never let on. In fact, after everything I learned about my own body, I learned a few things about Phillip's, too, and that's when I started *him* on supplements. He trusts my research and hard work so much that he takes whatever I suggest (and feels a lot better for it), and he even lets me drag him to have his blood drawn every once in a while.

Robin's Rx Today, I've found wonderful doctors to help me manage my hormones, but when I was shopping around for the right expert, here are some things that helped then and still help me today:

- Ask questions in advance. Since I knew I wanted to take only natural hormones, the first question I'd ask before making an appointment was how the doctor felt about natural versus synthetic hormones.
- Prepare for the appointment. I bring a list of my concerns and symptoms and even notes on any symptoms I've experienced such as when they occurred and what they felt like. Also, bring up general concerns such as why

you wake up feeling sluggish (I personally like to hit the ground running in the morning and if that doesn't happen I want to know why).

- Listen carefully. It's important to pay attention to what the doctor says about how to use prescriptions. Sometimes the pharmacy will put "as needed" instead of specific directions.

- Do your research. Even if I trust the doctor immensely, I come home and research his or her suggestions. If you're not comfortable with your doctor's suggestions or don't understand them, ask him or her questions, get a second opinion, and talk to other women experiencing what you are.

- Move on if it's not a match. If you don't like a doctor, there's no harm in finding someone else. (Your health is too important to worry about hurting someone else's feelings.)

When we moved to California almost six and a half years ago, I had my hormones under control, but in order to keep it that way, I immediately started looking for a natural hormone therapy practitioner. Over the first four or five years, I met with several doctors and though I liked some of them, I never felt totally satisfied, so I kept looking. Now, when I'm trying to find an expert (be it a doctor or hairstylist), I network until I find what I'm looking for. So at the risk of driving other people crazy, I'm always asking questions of other women I meet. Over a year ago, I was getting my hair cut by a new gal named Lainie. I knew she was forty-four years old and noticed that she had such fabulous energy and optimism and was in fabulous shape. *She must be doing something right*, I thought, so I asked her how she managed hormones. When she told me about her natural regimen from The Hall Center in Santa Monica, where they specialize in managing hormone imbalances, inflammation, adrenal stress, and metabolic problems. I was so intrigued that I called them that day.

Robin's Rx Listen to your body! One way I do this is during prayer or meditation I try to get an image or feeling of how I would like my body to feel. We always visualize how we want to look, but never how we want to feel. This really gives you a good sense of what you're striving for and can help you verbalize how you're feeling (or how you want to feel and what's missing) to your doctor or health care professional.

At my appointment, I met Prudence Hall, MD, Founder and Medical Director of The Hall Center, specializing in Gynecology and Functional Medicine, and Howard Liebowitz, MD, Medical Director of The Hall Center specializing in Functional Medicine, Anti-Aging Medicine and Alternative Internal Medicine. "Our goal is to replace missing hormones with natural bioidentical hormones and correct root causes rather than only treat superficial symptoms," Dr. Hall explained. "We also focus on appropriate diet, lifestyle, acupuncture, and physical therapies as needed." When she added that they "view their clients as advocates for their own well-being" and explained my test results like no one else ever had, I knew I was in the right place. After that first round of tests, Dr. Hall stood there as she read through the results of my blood work and said, "I'm shocked that you're not battling your weight because your estrogen levels are really low. That's a good testament to how hard you work out and that you eat right." (Yes, another reason to exercise besides fitting into your skinny jeans!)

"I *am* in good shape and watch what I eat," I said. "But actually, in the last few months, I've started to see a little roll around my waist that wasn't there before."

"Well, let's get rid of that," Dr. Hall said calmly and with a sense that what I was experiencing was not only normal but entirely manageable. I marveled at what a huge difference her attitude was from that of Dr. Gold. Dr. Hall and Dr. Liebowitz simply increased my natural estrogen and explained why this works to decrease that fat around the middle that many women experience during menopause. "When estrogen decreases during menopause, it can cause something called 'insulin resistance,' which means that the body doesn't metabolize sugars as efficiently as it used to," explained Dr. Liebowitz. "So when you eat sugar, it gets deposited as fat, making you gain weight in areas of the body where there are a lot of fat stores. For women one of these areas is the stomach. By increasing estrogen you can better metabolize sugar so this along with exercise and eating correctly can help reduce that roll around the middle." It worked for me. Not long after they increased my estrogen, I leaned out and felt better than I had in a while.

"Another reason for weight gain during menopause and changes in muscle and skin tone is decreasing levels of human growth hormone," added Dr. Liebowitz. Interestingly, I was born with a very high level of testosterone and human growth hormone. In fact, years ago, one of the first doctors I went to said he looked at my levels of this hormone and actually had the lab retest it because he thought they made a mistake. But it was no mistake and is one thing that has kept my skin from wrinkling, besides helping me stay lean and build muscle.

It's now been almost ten years since I started my journey through menopause. Looking back, I realize that the more I researched and learned, the more I gained a huge sense of control over my life and my body and the more I quelled any fears that I had about menopause. I know in the past our mothers and grandmothers talked in hushed tones about going through "the change," but I thought, *I'm not going to let this change me. I'm actually going to embrace menopause. Why shouldn't I when it's a very normal and natural part of the aging process that every woman on the planet is going to go through?* I decided to view it in a positive light as something, like pregnancy, that only woman get to experience. I thought, *This is my time for menopause. Maybe someone else my age won't go through it for ten years, but now is my time.* I saw menopause as an opportunity to take charge of my body and how I lived the rest of life.

I really want other women to feel the same way and that's one reason I am sharing my story. I want you, no matter your age, to look forward to this time without worrying that it's going to be life changing in a bad way. You simply need to do your research and arm yourself with the knowledge of what's going on and what you can do to make yourself feel your best. And that brings me to another point: you shouldn't wait until perimenopause or menopause to have your hormones evaluated. "Things like PMS, irregular or heavy periods, weight gain, or exhaustion can indicate either a hormone imbalance or thyroid problem," Jim explains. "These can be really overwhelming problems that interrupt your life and yet alleviating them may simply mean increasing a hormone that you're deficient in or balancing one that you're dominant in." That is one reason I want to make the point that it's not just women who are on the verge of menopause who need to educate themselves about their bodies and hormones. I think all women should.

Prior to the age of forty-five, I didn't know anything about how our hormone levels vary with each passing decade and how this can affect us, but I really wish I had. In that case, I would have started managing my hormone levels in my thirties. By getting blood work done and monitoring any changes, I likely would have been on a lot of supplements and natural hormones in my thirties and forties, and as a result, I probably wouldn't have experienced even one symptom of menopause. Even so, I've been in menopause from the age of forty-five until now and yet, because of all the supplements and natural hormones I've been taking, I have barely suffered.

I took my thirty-year-old daughter-in-law, Erica, and her two sisters (they're triplets) to have their blood work done, and now they are all managing their hormones. Like many women their age, they thought they were exhausted because they're busy young women with careers and families. They accepted being tired as a part of life—especially because all their friends felt the same way. But just because we all feel one way doesn't mean it's okay. Results of their blood work revealed that the fatigue Erica and her sisters were willing to accept as a natural part of life in their thirties wasn't natural at all. Turns out they all have low thyroids. Now they're taking natural hormones and feel better than they have in years. (So much so, that they convinced their mother to fly to California from the Midwest to have her blood work done at The Hall Center too.)

The other reason I think we all need to educate ourselves about perimenopause and menopause in advance is that it comes on at different times (and can last anywhere from one to ten years) and with an array of different symptoms for each women. That means that you probably won't go through it at the same time as your best friends or sisters (which is what happened to me); and even if you do, your experience can be quite different. Most of us think we'll know that we're in menopause because it's a time when your period stops. However, when you're in perimenopause, you can have several symptoms and still be having a period so that you never even dream it's got anything to do with menopause! This is true for a lot of women and is why so many of us are suffering with "just not feeling right" but don't know why. If this is you, you're not alone. I was amazed recently when I met a woman named Lisa who was actually a doctor who had been going through menopause for years and didn't realize it. Here's what happened: Lisa and I were seated next to one another at a dinner party. The host was about to open the door to the patio and asked us, "Is that okay? Or will you be too cold?"

"Cold?" Lisa exclaimed. "I haven't been cold in ten years!" It was then that I noticed that she had really dark circles under her eyes and a very dull, dry complexion. Earlier in the evening, she complained about feeling tired and lethargic. Like a detective putting clues together, my mind started racing and I just couldn't help but ask her a few questions when we were alone later that night. "I don't mean to be nosy, but can I ask you something?"

"Sure," Lisa replied.

"Do you do anything to manage your hormones?" She shook her head no.

"Do you still get your period?"

"Yes," she said. "In fact, except for three years ago when I didn't have one for a few months, it's still very consistent."

"Do you have a headache every day at three o'clock?"

"Yes," she said. "How did you know?"

"I think you should go have your blood work done, because I bet you're in perimenopause. I really don't think there's any reason for you to suffer like you are." That's when she told me that she was in fact a doctor. I was amazed. I wasn't amazed, however, when she called me after her appointment at The Hall Center and said that they found that she was in menopause and that her hormones and thyroid were off.

I know some people would call me nosy, but what I really am is passionate about being a woman and helping other women feel their best. It's all too easy to let a few symptoms become a normal part of our daily lives. But the truth is, life is hard enough as it is. A little fatigue or weight gain here or irritability or bloating there makes it even harder, and it doesn't have to be that way. So when it comes to menopause or any other health issue, I urge you to be proactive. You don't have to sit and suffer through feeling bad.

There's always something you can do about it; you just have to take action. For example, I have a close friend who recently told me that she was battling her weight and found herself sitting at home crying all the time. My first reaction was, "And that's okay with you?" Of course, it wasn't okay with her, but she accepted it because she didn't realize that she had another option. Sometimes we're so used to how bad we feel or see so many other women experiencing the same thing that we actually think it's normal.

This also happened years go with my niece, who was twenty-six years old at the time. She was at my house with her eight-week-old baby and was talking about how drained and exhausted she felt. Then she said, "But of course, it's normal that I'm tired. After all, I just had a baby." "Actually, it's not that normal and you don't have to accept being tired just because you're a new mother." Now of course, we're all worn out when our kids are little, but why not do everything you can to feel your best in spite of that? As a result of our conversation, my niece went to her doctor and found out that her thyroid was really low. Sure, she was tired from her busy life. But she was even *further* behind the eight ball because of her thyroid. With just a little supplementation, she was at least playing with a full deck. A lot of women are guilty of saying, "I'm busy with kids and life. No wonder I'm irritable, I don't sleep (or I'm fat)." But it doesn't have to be that way. We don't have to make excuses for how we feel. It's time to take control and take those small steps to feel better.

Trust me, you'll never regret taking a step forward toward good health, and you'll feel such a sense of empowerment from doing just that. That's exactly how I feel. Rather than simply being patient number 346 who left Dr. Gold's office ten years ago and obligingly filled that stack of prescriptions, I took control over my body. I did my homework and I can honestly say that I had a very positive experience because I was prepared for it. My transition into and through menopause couldn't have been smoother. I never had a horrible, severe stage, and I know all this work and focus on my health is one reason why at fifty-five years old, I pretty much eat what I want, sleep well, have endless energy, and despite normal fluctuations, my weight is stable. My body and health are working for me and I feel better than I ever have. I know that you can feel that way, too, no matter how old you are!

Answers from the Experts

Jim Hrncir, RPh, of Las Colinas Pharmacy Compounding and Wellness Center in Irving, Texas, www.lascolinaspharmacy.com.

Prudence Hall, MD, Founder and Medical Director of The Hall Center in Santa Monica, California specializing in Gynecology and Functional Medicine.

Howard Liebowitz, MD, Medical Director of The Hall Center in Santa Monica California specializing in Functional Medicine, Anti-Aging Medicine and Alternative Internal Medicine.

Frank Lawlis, PhD, psychologist, sleep expert, and author of *The Stress Answer* and *The IQ Answer*.

How do I know if my thyroid is off?

Your thyroid gland, which is located at the base of your neck, is a small, powerful hormone center that regulates your metabolism and controls your body temperature, digestion, and other hormones throughout the body. Low thyroid, an often undiagnosed condition, is called hypothyroid disease, and symptoms include fatigue, low sex drive, weight gain, brittle nails, constipation, poor memory and concentration, dry, rough skin, depression, hair loss, frequent sweating, prominent bags under the eyes, high cholesterol (in spite of a healthy diet), difficult menopause symptoms, muscle aches and pains, irregular periods, infertility, cold hands and feet, difficulty getting going in the morning, and a feeling of being foggy-headed.

If you have more than eight of the above symptoms, the following Basal Body Test may help you figure out if you have a low thyroid.

- What you'll need: a basal body thermometer, available at most pharmacies.
- When to do it: If you're not menopausal, perform this test during the first few days of your period. (If you're menopausal, any day is fine.) Take your temperature first-thing in the morning, before doing *anything* else such as getting up to go to the bathroom, brushing your teeth, or moving around.
- How: Place the end of the thermometer under your bare armpit while you lie on your side and keep it there for about three or four minutes. Perform this test for several days in a row, and record the readings each time (you may think you'll remember, but writing it down is important).

  day 1 _____
  day 2 _____
  day 3 _____
  day 4 _____

- What it means: Add together the 4 total values and divide by 4 to get an average. Ninety-eight degrees is a normal, average reading. One degree less than this is indicative of low thyroid, so talk your doctor or health care provider.

What supplements can I take to help with menopause?

Supplements are a good idea, but it's important to remember that they're just one part of a natural approach to menopause that also includes good nutrition, exercise, and bio-identical hormones. Below are some of the supplements that help with menopause and what they do for the body. Arm yourself with this information and then talk to your doctor about which ones are right for you. Never take anything new without talking to a health care expert, because it's important to make sure it doesn't interact with anything else you're taking and that it's right for your body. Also note that none of these supplements is a cure for your symptoms but rather provides a short-term solution. In order to get rid of or reduce your symptoms over the long term, it's important to have your hormones evaluated and balanced by a professional.

- Fish oil has an overall anti-inflammatory effect throughout the body and can affect brain functioning. It may also have an indirect impact on hot flashes.

- Evening primrose oil is an omega-6 fatty acid that some authorities believe may stimulate extra production of progesterone in women who have lost some of this hormone. Based on that assumption, it may help alleviate breast tenderness, mood swings, anxiety, irritability, headaches, and water retention.

- Magnesium and calcium may have a tonic affect on the nervous system and help to relieve mood swings, insomnia, and anxiety.

- L-theonine is a tea derivative that may have a calming effect on the body without causing drowsiness. Research on medical students showed those students who took l-theonine did better on exams and felt calmer and more focused.

- The following, taken in very small doses, may help with hot flashes. However, make sure to take them under the care of a homeopathic expert, because too much of any of these remedies or taking more than one at a time can have the opposite effect. Sepia, lachesis mutus, and glonoinum may help with hot flashes as well as anxiety and tension associated with menopause. Belladonna can help with perspiration.

I never had any problems sleeping until I hit menopause. Can there be a connection between the two?

Definitely. Insomnia is common during perimenopause and menopause because the loss of estrogen stimulates the adrenal glands in a stress response. This disrupts the body's natural circadian rhythms (which is the body's internal clock that regulates various biological processes) and upsets the delicate balance of the hormones that are secreted by the pituitary and pineal glands at night. Once this delicate balance is upset, sleep becomes very difficult. Furthermore, many women experience symptoms like hot flashes and night sweats from the loss of estrogen, and this can wake you up at night as well as reduce the quality of your sleep.

Unfortunately, chronic sleep deprivation is problematic. Our bodies and minds renew themselves when we're in the deepest stages of sleep (called stages three and four). It's here that, among other things, the pituitary gland releases a pulse of growth hormones that stimulate tissue and muscle repair, and blood levels of substances that activate the immune system increase and levels of the stress hormone cortisol decline so your adrenal glands, which pump out this hormone, get a much-needed rest. Even the skin restores itself as it turns over its cells. Yet, if you can't fall asleep or keep waking up, your body may not reach these stages. Because all of your organs, cells, tissues, and muscles don't get a chance to restore themselves, they can wear out and you may age more quickly. Additionally, worn out and depleted adrenal glands can bring on or worsen menopausal symptoms and the higher levels of the stress hormone cortisol that are floating around your body can negatively impact your metabolism possibly causing weight gain, high cholesterol, and preventing nutrients from your food from getting where they need to in the body. Sleep deprivation also affects your problem-solving skills, alertness, and performance.

Restoring the hormones in the same cyclical pattern that they had before menopause will allow you to get back into a normal circadian rhythm and sleep again. However, there are several other things that you can do to improve the quality of your sleep:

- Dress in lightweight pajamas, use a light blanket and put on a fan or air-conditioning to help with hot flashes.
- Don't drink alcohol before bed. It may help you nod off at first, but it can actually wake you during the night and prevent you from getting to the restorative stages of sleep. The same thing may happen if you take certain sleep medications.
- Avoid sugar prior to going to sleep, and stop drinking caffeine by late afternoon because it can stay in your system for hours.
- Count backward seven to nine hours from the time you have to wake up in the morning and make that your bedtime. By going to bed at the same time each night, your body adjusts and starts producing melatonin, a hormone that induces sleepiness.
- Use your bed for sex and sleep—not things like work, paying bills, talking on the phone, or arguments.
- Have a bedtime routine, which helps signal to your body that it's time to go to sleep. This can be as simple as a bath or a cup of tea and prayer.
- Dim the lights and avoid light from the TV or computer at least a half an hour before bed. Light to the eyes affects our natural circadian rhythms and wakes us up.
- Stress and anxiety can keep you up at night or make it hard to fall asleep. Figure out what relaxes you—be it journaling, prayer, a few yoga stretches—and do this before you turn in for the night.
- The ideal room to sleep in is one that is cool, dark, and quiet.
- Take a nap if you're tired during the day. Just keep it brief since research shows that thirty minutes is the optimal amount of time to nap, and any longer than that can cause grogginess.

- Exercise is believed to help you sleep more deeply; just make sure to do so at least three hours before bedtime.

What are symptoms of imbalanced hormones?

Here are specific symptom checklists that experts use in conjunction with blood work to determine if there are hormone imbalances. (This is important to note since the body is extremely complex with lots of systems interacting and using symptoms alone to diagnose can be quite confusing.) Once you complete the checklist, your responses will suggest the areas of imbalance that may need to be investigated. Then, you and your doctor or health care provider will have a clearer idea about where to start in relation to lab work and prescriptions.

Symptoms of low or imbalanced estrogen

Check any of the following that you experience:

- ☐ Difficulty falling asleep
- ☐ Forgetfulness
- ☐ Mental fogginess
- ☐ Minor anxiety
- ☐ Mood change
- ☐ Hot flashes
- ☐ Night sweats
- ☐ Temperature swings
- ☐ Daylong fatigue
- ☐ Reduced stamina
- ☐ Decreased sense of sexuality or sensuality
- ☐ Lessened self-image and attention to appearance
- ☐ Dry eyes, skin, and vagina

☐ Loss of skin radiance

☐ Sense of normalcy only during second week of cycle

☐ Sagging breasts and loss of breast fullness

☐ Pain with sexual activity

☐ Weight gain with increasing lack of concern about it

☐ Increased back and joint pain

☐ Episodes of rapid heartbeat with or without anxiety

☐ Headaches and migraines

☐ Gastrointestinal discomfort

☐ Decreased bladder control

☐ Water retention

☐ Tender breasts

☐ Feeling uptight and irritated, but with a clear mind

☐ Pelvic cramps

☐ Nausea

Symptoms of low progesterone

Check any of the following that you experience:

☐ Infrequent period, such as every 3 to 4 months

☐ Heavy and frequent periods

☐ Spotting a few days before period

☐ PMS

☐ Cystic breasts

☐ Painful breasts

☐ Breasts with lumps

☐ Endometriosis, fibroids, and adenomyosis

☐ Anxiety, irritability, and nervousness

☐ Water retention

Symptoms of low testosterone

Check any of the following that you experience:

☐ Flabbiness and muscular weakness

☐ Lack of energy and stamina

☐ Loss of coordination and balance

☐ Loss of sense of security

☐ Indecisiveness

☐ Decreased sex drive

☐ Poor body image

☐ Decreased armpit, pubic, and body hair

Symptoms of low DHEA

Check any of the following that you experience:

☐ Stress

☐ Lack of stamina

☐ Intolerance of loud noises

☐ Constant fatigue

☐ Poor mood

☐ Decreased immunity

☐ Memory loss

☐ Loss of pubic hair

☐ Poor abdominal muscle support

☐ Dry skin and eyes

☐ Poor sex drive

Symptoms of polycystic ovarian syndrome

Check any of the following that you experience:

☐ Scalp hair loss

☐ Increased facial, arm, and leg hair

- ☐ Edema
- ☐ Increased acne and skin redness
- ☐ Decreased fertility and increased miscarriages
- ☐ Increased musculature and weight gain
- ☐ Insulin resistance

Which are the most commonly used human bio-identical hormones?

The most commonly used bio-identical hormones are listed below. However, it's important to note that though you may see over-the-counter versions of progesterone, DHEA, and pregnenalone, these versions are actually illegal according to the Food and Drug Administration (FDA). As mentioned earlier, it's best to see a doctor who prescribes the following in order to make sure your hormones are balanced and monitored:

- Estradiol, which is the most potent human estrogen, is helpful in controlling hot flashes, reducing "mental fogginess," stimulating endometrial tissue in the uterus, and reducing bone loss.
- Estriol, which is thought to be protective against breast cancer and helpful in vaginal lubrication and mental fogginess.
- Estrone, which is thought to be responsible for the greatest risk of breast cancer due to its metabolites.
- Progesterone, which helps strengthen bones and balance estrogen, is believed to protect against all types of cancer, including breast and uterine cancer and heart disease, and can have a calming effect.
- Testosterone, which is thought to down-regulate estrogen receptors in breast tissue, leading experts to believe it may reduce breast cancer risks. It is also helpful in increasing libido, metabolism, and brain function.

- DHEA and Pregnenalone, which are hormones that the body converts to estrogen, progesterone, and testosterone. The appropriate levels help normalize the metabolism, provide hormonal balance, strengthen the immune system and adrenal glands and improve both brain function and adrenal support.

I've heard that it isn't a good idea to eat a lot of soy during menopause. Is that true?

The evidence surrounding whether or not eating soy is beneficial or harmful for women in menopause is at best inconclusive. There are some studies that claim that the estrogen-like effect of soy can help reduce hot flashes, while other studies and specialist opinions indicate that increased soy consumption may increase the risk of breast cancer. The bottom line is that there's really no good evidence on either side to support these assumptions. (However, for men there is some indication that eating too much soy protein can upset the ideal balance between estrogen and testosterone.)

Generally, some experts at The Hall Center advise that both men and women avoid processed soy products such as tofu, tempeh, and soy milk products since it's believed that the processing of soy creates an inferior artificial-like protein. However, something like whole natural edamame beans is okay. (Soy protein is also known as one of the more common food intolerances along with dairy, wheat, and eggs, so if this is an issue for you, you may want to avoid it for this reason.)

I'm worried about my breast cancer risk since hitting menopause. How can I lower my risks?

There are several important things you can do both pre-, post-, and during menopause:

- Maintain balanced "bio-identical" hormones.
- Exercise regularly.
- Eat at least three servings of cruciferous vegetables each week. These include broccoli, Brussels sprouts, cabbage, and cauliflower.
- Take supplements Indole-3 carbamide or 3-3 diindolemethane (DIM).
- Include antioxidants such as Co-enzyme Q-10, selenium, folic acid, vitamin E, vitamin C, and green tea polyphenols in your diet.
- Decrease your exposure to what are called xenoestrogens, which are things like chlorine, pesticides, PCBs and plasticizers. You can do so by washing fruits and vegetables well, buying organic produce, buying organic and free-range chicken and beef and "wild caught" cold water fish if possible, drinking bottled water that is naturally chlorine free, and not drinking hot liquids from soft plastic or Styrofoam containers.

What are the top things that I can do to prevent heart disease before, during, or after menopause?

- Know your cholesterol and blood pressure, two leading risk factors for heart disease that have no symptoms. You need to have not only your total cholesterol tested, but your LDL (low-density lipoprotein, or "bad") cholesterol, HDL (high-density lipoprotein or "good") cholesterol, and triglycerides (another type of fat in the blood associated with HDL, obesity, diabetes, and high blood pressure). For total cholesterol, your number should be under 200 mg/dl, with an LDL less than 100 mg/dl and HDL of 50 mg/dl or higher. Your blood pressure reading should be 120/80 mmHg.
- Quit smoking because nicotine puts a lot of stress on the blood vessels, deprives your body of oxygen, and speeds up the buildup of

plaque in your arteries. If you smoke, your risk of heart disease is two to four times greater than that of a nonsmoker, and if you have a heart attack you're more likely to die and die suddenly (within an hour) than a woman who doesn't smoke. Your risk of a blood clot goes up even more if you smoke and take birth control pills.

- Try to control your weight, especially if you carry excess fat around your middle. Fat around your waist can interfere with your metabolism, increasing your risk of diabetes and negatively affecting your cholesterol.

- Exercise regularly. Researchers at Harvard Medical School looked at more than twenty-seven thousand women and found that just one to two hours of exercise per week reduced their risk of heart disease by 27 percent, two to five hours per week reduced their risk by 32 percent, and more than five hours decreased the women's risk by 41 percent.[2]

- Know your family history. Heredity is a big risk factor for heart disease, but you shouldn't just know how healthy your parents' hearts are (or were). Some research suggests that having a brother or sister with heart disease may be an even bigger predictor of whether you'll develop it yourself.[3]

- Avoid trans and saturated fats, which can clog arteries, lower good cholesterol, and raise bad cholesterol.

- Be aware that signs of a heart attack are different for women than men. Just 50 percent of women have chest pain, so watch for other symptoms, which can include pain in your arm, jaw, neck, or back, terrible nausea, dizziness and/or vomiting, sweating, and shortness of breath.

- If you suspect you're having a heart attack, get help ASAP. The symptoms are often subtle or can be confused with other illnesses, so you may be reluctant to go to the ER or your doctor. But better safe than sorry because how quickly you get to the hospital after a heart attack has a huge impact on your recovery and survival. Though that first hour is critical in terms of having treatments to open up clogged arteries and restore blood circulation, studies suggest that two-thirds of women who have a heart attack never make it to the hospital.

6

What's Hair
Got to Do with It?

"Cut it all off," I told Debbie, my stylist at a local Dallas beauty shop.

"What?" she said. She sounded startled—and with good reason. About every six weeks for the last five years, she'd given me an adorable few-inches-below-the-shoulders haircut and I'd loved it. For me to say, "Cut it off" was shocking for her.

"I just turned forty, so I guess it's time to go short," I said.

The first time I'd cut my hair short was when I was five years old, and I wore it that way until I was about twelve. Back then our family didn't have a lot of money, and a little pixie style was one of the few that they did at the least expensive salon in town. When I was finally allowed to grow my hair long like my three older sisters, I was thrilled; and from then on it was always somewhere between the middle of my back and my shoulders. But having recently blown out forty candles on my birthday cake, I thought it was time to adhere to that unwritten rule that women over a certain age can't wear long hair. *I'm a real adult now,* I thought, *so I guess I need to look like one.* With me urging her along, Debbie started chopping away at my thick, brown locks until long strands lay on the floor at her feet. By the end, my hair was in a little bob style about an inch above my jaw line. It was so short that I couldn't even tuck it behind my ears. As a haircut, it was stylish and cute; on me, well, not so much.

Just hours later, I met up with Phillip at one of Jay's football games. He didn't know that I was planning to cut my hair, so his eyes grew wide when he saw me climbing up the stairs toward where he was sitting in the bleachers. "New hairdo," he said.

"Yes," I replied. "You're not supposed to have long hair at my age."

Phillip nodded as if what I'd just said made complete sense. "Well, I prefer it longer, but what matters is that *you* like it." (That kind of blessed tact is what you get from marrying a man with three sisters!) "But," he added, "you sure are cute." I smiled at this comment—one that he says often to remind me that whether my hair is short, long, or bald, what I look like doesn't really matter to him as long as I'm the same person on the inside.

Then the football game started and Jay came out onto the field. Like always, I saw him peer up into the stands scanning the seats for Phillip and me. This time, I watched his jaw drop when he zeroed in on us. He mouthed the word, "Mom!" as he pointed to his hair and shook his head as if to say, "What have you done?" Imagine, this kid was just fourteen years old, and even *he* had the wherewithal to know that short hair and Robin McGraw don't mix! He wasn't the only one. Nobody said outright that they didn't like my haircut. Instead, they made comments like, "Oh, you cut your hair" (as if I didn't know!) or "Wow, short hair!"

Lucky for me, my hair grows very quickly (to this day, I have to trim my bangs weekly and get color every three weeks or I have very noticeable roots.) As a result, I've never really panicked over a bad haircut or color (more of those stories in the pages to come). Still, I hated my short 'do so much that even my hair's speedy growth rate was not fast enough, so I relied on a trick that I swear works: I went to the health food store and got supplements made for hair and popped these along with my usual multi-vitamin. Though some experts are skeptical about whether or not vitamins can really impact hair growth, I personally believe that it's helpful to give your strands the nutrition they need (and when you hate a haircut, even the placebo effect is a welcomed one!) The vitamins and minerals typically thought to be important for hair include niacin, folic acid, biotin, calcium, zinc, and coenzymes. (Just make sure to check with your doctor, like I did, before taking these.)

After every bad experience in my life, big or small, I always pause and ask myself what I've learned. That unflattering short bob taught me two things. The first and most obvious: I will never cut my hair off again. The second and more important lesson: age shouldn't dictate how you wear your hair. Instead, you have to look and care for yourself in a way that makes you happy, rather than follow some unwritten rules or preconceived ideas.

Today, I'm fifty-five years old and my hair is actually longer than it has ever been, and it will stay long well into my sixties, seventies, and eighties. It's taken me a long time to figure out what style works best for me, but I know that short hair doesn't fit my face or the structure of my jaw line and that I plan to have long hair whether I'm rocking my future grand-children in my arms or, God willing, dancing at their weddings. Now that doesn't mean I don't envy short hair. In fact, I've seen women with the most precious close-cropped cuts that I wish I could wear. Even my own mother had an adorable short hairdo that looked fabulous on her, but would look awful on me. But the bottom line is that your hair shouldn't have anything to do with how many birthdays you've celebrated or what's "in" at the moment; it has to do with what you like best and feel most comfortable with.

Unfortunately, that super-short bob wasn't my only hair disaster. I've had two not-so-pretty experiences with the wrong color, the worst of which happened when I was first dating Phillip in my early twenties. One day, his mother and I were sitting around her kitchen table chatting. "You have such gorgeous, thick hair," she said, twirling a strand of it around her finger. "It would look beautiful if it were blonde."

"Really?" I said. "I've never thought of that." In the past, I'd experimented with various cuts and hair colors, but blonde was never one of them.

"Oh yes! Especially with your eyes," she said. "Let's call the girl who does my hair and see when she can fit you in." Excited at the prospect of change, I called and made an appointment for the next day, a Tuesday, which was my day off. When I arrived at the salon around 8:00 a.m., the colorist washed and conditioned my hair, applied the bleach, and tucked my hair under a cap. Every hour on the hour, she'd come over to see if my brown locks were now blonde. At first it didn't seem strange that it was taking a long time for the color to take. After all, my hair was down to the middle of my back so I knew it would take a while. But as the hours ticked by, I could tell her expression was one of concern. My hair was so thick that it was just not taking the bleach. By 6:00 p.m., my scalp was covered in painful sores and all I wanted was to get out of that chair. "I can't do one more thing to your hair or it will fall out," the stylist said. Visions of me with Phillip's bald head (yes, he was bald even back in our twenties!) danced in my mind. "You'll have to come back tomorrow for me to put the toner on."

"I have to work tomorrow," I told her. "I can't come back until my day off, which is a week from today." Without the toner my hair was a bright, bleached blonde (think Pamela Anderson). It also looked huge! When you color your hair, the pigment or bleach gets into the cuticle, causing the hair shaft to swell so it normally looks a little bit thicker than usual (which is why coloring can be a good option for women with thin hair). However, I have so much hair to begin with that it looked enormous. (I guess, lucky for me, huge hair was actually "in" back in Texas.) I still lived with my parents at the time, and my father looked shocked when I walked in the door. "What did you *do*?" he asked. I'd like to say that he was the only one with that shocked reaction, but he wasn't. Everyone in my life from Phillip to my coworkers to the checkout girl at the grocery store asked me the same question. Still, I rationalized that it would look much better in a week when I had the toner on. By the time my appointment rolled around, I was not only eager to quiet my very unnatural looking color, but freaked out by what appeared to be little dark ants sitting on my scalp.

"What *are* these?" I asked the colorist, pointing to my head.

"Honey, that's what we call roots!" she said. "You're going to have to come in more often than I thought to have them touched up because your hair grows so fast." She finished up with the toner, and though on its own the color was beautiful, it wasn't me. At all!

I also realized that I couldn't afford the time or money necessary for monthly root touch-ups (future maintenance is something important to consider before making any drastic changes to your hair), so just days later I found myself back in the salon begging for my old color—or as close as I could get. Though it went from blonde to brown within an afternoon, my hair was never exactly the same, and I spent over a year repeatedly dying and trimming my hair until the blonde grew out. At the time, I was so upset with myself for putting my poor hair and head through all that trauma, but nothing compares to how horrible Phillip's mother felt for encouraging me. I never blamed her (hey, I was the one who dialed the salon for the appointment and sat in that chair), but at least it's a story that gives us a really good laugh today.

I should have learned my lesson about doing things on a whim back then, but I didn't. Just a few years after the bad fortieth birthday bob, I made another hair color mistake. In my late twenties, I had discovered highlights and loved how they gave my hair a little dimension and lift. My favorites are true blonde streaks on top of my head and bangs, but not all over. I've had some great highlights over the years and I love Lucie Doughty, the woman who does my color now. But I've also had some bad ones, which brings me to my most recent—and hopefully last—bad hair story.

It was a Sunday afternoon when, on a whim, I decided that I really wanted to have a few more highlights in the front of my hair. My regular colorist had been out of town for a while, so I called over to a well-known salon in my Dallas neighborhood and was thrilled when they said that, yes, they had an appointment available that afternoon. Unfortunately, that feeling of elation evaporated as soon as the colorist removed the foil from my hair revealing horrible, bright white stripes on my otherwise brown hair. *What have I done?* I thought. *And why didn't I just wait for my usual colorist to come back to town?*

The next day, I had a bunch of women at my house helping me with a project for Jordan's class. "Look what I did," I said, pointing to the white streaks in my hair. "I'm going to have to learn to stop doing things on a whim."

"My husband Joe owns a salon, and since it's Monday, he's off," one of the women said. "If you want, I can call him and see if he can fix it."

"If it's not a problem, I'd love it!" I exclaimed. Even though I barely knew her and had never met her husband, it seemed like the perfect solution. When I met up with Joe at his salon, I explained that I simply wanted to cover up the highlights with a color similar to my hair. I believed him when he said he understood, but I guess I should have been both more clear and less trusting because I emerged from his salon with jet black hair. Yes, jet black, which looked even darker and harsher against my pale skin! When Jay and Jordan came home from school, they took one look at me and broke down in pure, stomach-clenching hysterics. I laughed along with them and said, "Just call me Elvira!" After all, being ever the optimist, I thought I could simply wash the awful color out of my hair. Right? Oh so wrong! Five shampoos later, I looked as much like Elvira as I did when I got home. (And I realized that even the white, chunky highlights looked better than this!) I called Joe, asked him what he'd used on my hair, and nearly fell over when he said it was permanent color, which means that it doesn't wash out, but actually has to grow out! (This is unlike demi- or semi-permanent color which rinses out after eight to twenty-four shampoos.)

Feeling totally desperate, I hid my hair under a baseball cap and went to the store to pick up Palmolive dish soap and Prell shampoo, a combination that I remembered hearing could strip hair. Back at home, I mixed them up and got in the shower, but after six additional shampoos, not a strand on my head had changed color. Though Jay and Jordan still found my jet-black locks absolutely hilarious, I wasn't laughing anymore. There was nothing funny about being so impatient for change that I couldn't wait for my usual hair stylist (experimenting is one thing; making rash, uninformed decisions is another that I would not recommend). After all that showering, I threw on an old terrycloth romper, dried my hair, and set about making dinner. *At least I don't have to go out of the house for the rest of the day,* I thought, *so no one will see me.* Boy, was I wrong!

So here's the ridiculous end to a ridiculous story. At the time, we lived on a golf course and were very good friends with the golf pro Paul Earnest. I looked out a window at the back of the house, and noticed that not only was Paul playing on the hole right behind of our house, but he and a golfing companion were walking off the course, coming around to the front door and—ding-dong—ringing my doorbell! With no other choice, I answered the door. *He probably won't even notice my hair,* I thought. *How bad could this be?* Here's how bad: I opened the door and there standing with Paul was Michael Bolton. Yes, *the* Michael Bolton! To make matters worse, this was right when he'd cut his long hair into that absolutely gorgeous cropped hair cut. (I'm sure you know the one I'm talking about!)

"Robin, I hope we're not bothering you," Paul said. "But Michael was admiring your house from the outside and I thought if you were home he could take a quick look inside too."

"Sure," I said, stunned that I was standing before *the* Michael Bolton who happened to look gorgeous. And I mean absolutely gorgeous in a black golf shirt and black pants with his golden tan and beautiful eyes. This was in stark contrast to me standing there in an old, ratty, terrycloth romper with no makeup and jet-black Elvira hair. "Come in and take a look."

"Thanks a lot," Michael said stepping over the threshold. "And next time your husband goes to see Oprah, please have him say hello for me."

"Actually, Phillip's leaving for Chicago tonight, so he'll see her tomorrow."

"Really?" Michael said. "Can I write her a note and have him pass it on?"

"Sure. But, just one thing before you take another step," I said. And then I pointed to my hair. "I have to tell you that this is a hair appointment gone bad. My hair is usually not this color." Yes, it sounds vain. Actually, it *is* vain. But when Michael Bolton is standing in your kitchen looking better than he ever has—in my humble opinion—and you're standing there looking worse than you ever have, I think a little explanation is in order. He was sweet and tried to laugh it off saying, "Trust me, I've had my own hair issues so I know how you feel," but there was just no way he could under-stand my embarrassment. Over a year later, we saw him at the premiere of Oprah's movie *Beloved* in New York City when my hair was back to normal.

He and Phillip were chatting when he reached his hand out to me and said, "Nice to meet you."

"Actually, we've met before," I said. He looked perplexed so I continued: "At our house in Dallas when you were playing golf with Paul."

"*That* was you?" Michael said with surprise in his voice. Now usually it's beyond insulting when someone you've already met doesn't remember you. This time it was the best compliment ever. And of course, the moral to that story is to take a deep breath and step away from the salon or the bottle of permanent hair color if you're changing your hair because you're bored or impatient.

With hair disaster number three under my belt, I became more careful about who I let cut and color my hair and how I communicated with them. Like most things in life, the key to finding a stylist and style that you really like is a little research. When I moved from Dallas to California, it took me five years to finally find the stylist and colorist I use today. I found them both by going up to women whose hair I liked and saying, "Who does your hair?" After a while, the same names kept coming up, and I knew I was on my way to a couple of winners.

You can also pop by a few local beauty shops and watch them do their work. If you stay just a little while, you'll see some real-life "before" and "after" cuts and get a sense if the salon is the place for you. Other times, you may be going to the right salon, but seeing the wrong stylist. If that's the case, don't be shy about switching to someone new. I've never had a problem doing this because I believe that when you're paying good money for your hair, you should get the results that you want. I've actually asked many stylists if it hurts their feelings or makes them mad when they see their client in someone else's chair. Amazingly, the results of my admittedly very unscientific study revealed that 80 to 90 percent said they'd rather a client be happy than stick with them out of guilt. So if you think the girl in the next chair's hair looks better than your own, approach her stylist and say, "I saw you do a great job on that woman. Will a similar cut or color work on me?" Communication is key, and any visual aids—I often bring pictures—can help. Also, once you know what you like, don't be afraid to speak up. For example, I've learned what I like best and have no problem telling my stylist that I like layering throughout my hair (it's too thick and heavy to be one length), long bangs (they cover my eyebrows, which I think are too far apart), and blonde highlights (copper and gold don't look good with the red in my hair).

Your daily hair-care routine and the products you use are also critical when it comes to keeping hair healthy. My daily routine depends on whether or not we're taping. On days when we tape the show, I shampoo and condition my hair with KeraStase Bain Satin 1 Complete Nutrition Shampoo and KeraStase Lait Vital Incredibly Light Nourishing Care Conditioner, which soften and smooth hair with ingredients like protein and lipids. (For years, I didn't use conditioner because I thought it was too heavy and that my natural oils were hydrating enough, but I learned that the right conditioner keeps hair soft, silky, and easy to style.) After rinsing with the coldest water I can stand, which helps close the cuticle so hair looks shiny and healthy, I get out of the shower, towel dry my hair, and brush it gently (wet hair is more fragile and prone to breakage so you need to handle it with care). Next, I apply KeraStase Mousse Nutri-Sculpt Bodifying Treatment Mousse and spend about fifteen minutes blow-drying the length of my hair with a round brush and my bangs with a flat brush. Both brushes contain a mix of plastic bristles, which help part the hair, and natural boar bristles, which help distribute the scalp's oils throughout the hair so it's shinier and smoother. After it's totally dry, I rub in a tiny drop of Fekkai Glossing Cream, a lightweight styling product that contains olive and grape seed oils.

Robin's Rx You may have heard that mayonnaise is a great way to condition your hair. But I think otherwise. One time when Phillip was traveling, I slathered it on my hair, covered it with a shower cap, and slept that way (I did it while he was away so he wouldn't have to smell or feel it). The next day it was so hard to rinse off and even after several shampoos my hair was greasy-looking for days. An easier, mess-free way to give hair shine is to apply regular hair conditioner on dry hair and put it in a ponytail before you work out. The heat your body generates while exercising helps open the cuticle, allowing the conditioner to penetrate. Then simply rinse in your post-exercise shower.

Here's my favorite trick for getting shine without the greasy look that can occur from using too much of any styling product: First, I rub the Fekkai Glossing Cream on my hands as if it's hand cream (and it does soften my skin because it's made with hydrating olive oil) and then when I barely have any left, I run my fingers through my hair. After this, I throw my hair into plastic Velcro rollers, which give it volume at the roots, a little body, and smoothness. Then, I apply my makeup, slip on a warm-up suit and pair of Uggs, and drive the twenty-five minutes from my house to the studio. Yes, you read that correctly, I drive to the studio with rollers in my hair. It may look silly (though so far I haven't been pulled over for indecent exposure or wound up in the tabloids like that), but if I take the rollers out beforehand, both the humidity and air make my hair flat as a board. Once at the studio, I remove the rollers, and occasionally I end by using a flat iron to tame the curly hairs that crop up around my ears.

Once I'm done, I meet with Mimi, the woman in charge of Phillip's hair and my own, who quickly checks to make sure that I don't have any pieces sticking up. This is important because the camera, especially HD, magnifies everything—so if there's just one teeny strand out of place, it's like there's a spotlight on it. In fact, this is exactly why guests often look different in the taped pieces done in their homes than they do when they appear in person on the *Dr. Phil* set. On the set, their hair is straightened as much as possible so that the camera doesn't pick up on any stray strands, whereas at home without the glare of the studio lights and cameras, it looks okay. I'm actually convinced that just like the camera adds ten pounds to the body, it does the same to the hair. There are times when I'll watch the show and realize that it looks like I teased my hair (something I've never needed to do thanks to the big, thick head of hair I was born with!).

We tape three shows in one day, so recently Mimi came up with the idea of using a curling iron on my hair between the shows. Though the curl I get from my rollers lasts through one show, by the time we're taping the second one, my hair is straight as a board. It's just so thick and heavy that it can't hold a curl. So Mimi touches it up with a curling iron and I just love the way it looks. I never realized what a good job a curling iron could do because for some reason, despite very good hand-eye coordination, I have never been able to work one. I'm not sure if it's because I'm left-handed or what, but the result is always hair that's creased or frizzy or the curling iron gets stuck.

When we're *not* taping the show, it's just like the days when I was a busy young mom, and I spend very little time on my hair. Back then I'd often slip on a baseball cap—especially to protect it from the hot, Texas sun. But today I simply twist my hair into a clip or pull it into a ponytail when I wake up—I just make sure that neither of these things is too tight since that can cause broken or thinning hair. (A pretty headband or casually tied scarf can do the trick too.) I shampoo my hair every two to three days because I don't want to rinse out my highlights and know that overwashing can strip hair of its naturally protective oils and increases the chances for breakage. If you've got curly hair, my colorist—Lucie—suggests that you use shampoo even less frequently—around once to twice a week if hair is fine and every two weeks if it's thick. Then every other time you climb into the shower, simply rinse hair with water and condition it starting in the middle of the hair to the ends. "Curly hair tends to lack moisture and feel more dry and brittle, so by rinsing you will not remove the natural oils, which can happen with shampooing," says Lucie. My hair doesn't get oily so it looks fine after a few days without being washed. If it doesn't look great, but I don't feel like washing my whole head, I simply shampoo my bangs under the faucet and blow them dry. For some reason, this makes the rest of my hair look perfectly clean and done.

Robin's Way

Robin's beautiful hair essentials:

- KeraStase Bain Satin Complete Nutrition shampoo
- KeraStase Lait Vital Incredibly Light Nourishing Care conditioner
- KeraStase Mousse Nutri-Sculpt
- Olivia Garden Ceramic + Ion Thermal Round Hair Brush
- Frederic Fekkai Classic Brush
- FHI Heat Blow-dryer
- Frederic Fekkai Glossing Cream

When it comes to my hair color, I've enjoyed experimenting with various shades since my twenties, but I started doing all-over color more regularly when my first gray hairs cropped up in my early forties. I was amazed to learn that hair is actually genetically predisposed to make less pigment at a certain age so you can't control when grays arrive. The good news is there's a lot you can do to blend or cover them. My colorist does just that with a permanent all-over color that she describes as "a mix of three colors that are a combination of brown shades with some gold for warmth and richness." On the ends she uses something called a demi-shine, which adds radiance and tone without adding color. It contains moisturizing agents and soy protein to hydrate this part of the hair, which because it's the oldest hair on the head, tends to be the driest. The lightener she uses for my blonde highlights has natural jojoba and sunflower oils so that my hair stays hydrated and shiny, rather than getting dry and brittle. (This is important since I color and highlight my hair almost every three weeks because it grows so fast.)

A lot of viewers have e-mailed me, asking if I think there's a time when they should just accept their gray hair and not color it anymore. Lucie believes that this is a really personal thing and that there's no set time or age when you all of a sudden have to let your hair go gray. "I think as we evolve, we become more in tune with our own style and how we feel best," says Lucie. I agree. If you want to go gray, I'm all for that, but you shouldn't stop coloring your hair because you've reached a certain age. Rather you should color or not color your hair depending on how you feel about your hair, the time and money that you have for upkeep, and what makes you feel most comfortable. Again, there are no rules.

If you do color your hair, Lucie suggests doing a few things to maintain that investment. This includes using shampoos, daily conditioners, and treatment products that are made for color-treated hair. They tend to be hydrating and gentle so they don't strip color and contain ingredients that protect against harsh UV rays and outside elements (which can fade and change colored hair faster than necessary). They are available at all price points from the drugstore aisle to the high-end hair salon, so you're bound to find one that's right for you. "If you invest your time and money into a great color, you should do the same with your products by picking those designed to work with your hair," adds Lucie. Also, occasional at-home or salon moisturizing treatments can help strengthen and protect hair. Lastly, get regular trims to keep hair looking healthy. You don't need to cut off a lot—even a quarter inch to remove the ends, which are the oldest and driest, can make hair look healthier and more vibrant.

Robin's Rx My daughter-in-law Erica and her two sisters, who are triplets, have been coloring their own hair at home for more than a decade now. Her biggest tip for women who also do this at home is to buy your hair color at a beauty supply store rather than a drugstore. "They have people there who test products and are really knowledgeable," she says. "They can help you find the right color or tweak your color if you don't like how it turned out."

The other critical part of my hair-care routine may seem to have nothing to do with my hair at all, but that is managing my hormones. Just like our skin changes with age, so does our hair. Some changes happen as a result of all the styling and chemical processing (like coloring, perming, and straightening) that we do to our hair over the years, but a lot of them are thanks to hormonal variations. "During perimenopause and menopause, many women complain that their hair is thinner, dryer, coarser, duller, or more brittle and less bouncy than it was when they were younger and some even experience balding," explains Howard Liebowitz, MD, Medical Director of The Hall Center in Santa Monica, California. "This is probably caused by the stress that the body goes through during menopause due to rapid hormonal and metabolic changes."

Plus, as we discussed in the chapter on skin, hormones work in the body as messengers telling the cells what to do. When estrogen levels decline, some cells in the body don't receive the signals needed to complete their functions "and this can include the cells in the hair that make moisture and oils," adds Liebowitz. "The good news is that the majority of women tell me that their hair improves (as well as their skin and nails) when they get their hormones balanced, especially with bio-identical hormones." I think because I started managing my hormones at the first sign of menopause, I didn't experience any changes in my hair. The exception to this was a few weeks when I was working on my thyroid and accidentally took three times as much of the bio-identical hormone DHEA, which increases testosterone in the body, than what my doctor suggested. Yes, three times! My skin broke out and my hair was thinning, but once I realized my mistake and scaled back on this supplement, my hair and skin went back to normal. (And, I learned to take notes and listen better at doctor's appointments.)

Lastly, I believe my hair is in great shape—both in general and for my age—because I never starved myself and eat a very balanced diet. This is really important because lack of certain nutrients can rob hair of its natural oils and the elements that create its support structures. In fact, I've heard experts say that when it comes to healthy, radiant hair (as well as skin and nails) there's nothing that you can apply topically that can remedy the impact of a poor diet. This is exactly why women who go on crash diets or with eating disorders like anorexia often have thinning, dry, and brittle hair.

What's crucial for healthy hair are good fats, which are the principle structural material of a living cell and make up about 3 percent of the hair shaft, such as omega-3 fatty acids found in nuts, flax, olive oil, salmon, and avocados. Without them hair can become parched and brittle and won't grow as fast. Another important food group is protein. Hair is made up of 65 to 95 percent protein, so it needs an adequate supply in order to grow and maintain its rich color. (As I've mentioned earlier, I love red meat and other protein like chicken, which is one reason I think my hair has never lost its bounce, shine, or volume.) Hair also requires iron, folic acid, and vitamins A, B C, D and E. "And drink plenty of water," adds Lucie. "If your body is well-hydrated, then your hair will benefit." Luckily, all the nutrients that are required for healthy hair are the same as those necessary for gorgeous skin and warding off disease, so looking beautiful from the inside out is actually pretty easy and doesn't require a diet overhaul.

Answers from the Expert

Lucie Doughty, celebrity colorist.

How can I find the best haircut to fit my face?

The ideal way is to have a consultation with a professional stylist. But it really helps to go into the salon with at least a sense of what you like. To do that, look through lots of magazines and photos of friends beforehand, and bring your favorites into the salon. Then during your meeting you can point to the pictures and say, "I like the bangs on the girl in this picture, but would like the length to be more like this picture." This gives the stylist an idea of what you're looking for (and she can tell you if it will work for your hair or not). To find a good stylist, ask around. In addition to talking to friends, if you see a woman on the street or at a party whose hair you love, don't be shy about going up to her and asking where she gets it done. She'll be flattered, and you might just find a haircut you love.

What causes thinning hair or hair loss?

It's actually normal to lose about 100 to 150 strands per day as our hair goes through the three stages of growth. Beyond that, several things can impact how thick or thin your hair is, though most of them are temporary and once remedied, your hair will usually go back to normal. These include:

- Pregnancy. At any one time, part of your hair is in a growth phase, a second part is in a resting phase, and a third is in a shedding phase. When you're pregnant, high levels of estrogen put more of your hair in the resting or growth phase so it can appear thicker. When these levels decrease from about ten weeks until about nine months postpartum, this extra hair starts shedding.

- Stress. Life events, illness, surgery, or rapid weight loss can also cause hair to stop growing. Normally about 90 percent of hair is in the growing phase while 10 percent is dormant. But if you're stressed out, the hair in the dormant stage can equal an amazing 60 percent.

- Hypothyroidism. When the body doesn't make enough thyroid hormone, and hair loss can be a symptom of this disease. See your doctor or health care provider if this is accompanied by other symptoms like fatigue, low sex drive, weight gain, brittle nails, constipation, poor memory and concentration, dry, rough skin, depression, frequent sweating, prominent bags under the eyes, high cholesterol (in spite of a healthy diet), difficult menopause symptoms, muscle aches and pains, irregular periods, infertility, cold hands and feet, difficulty getting going in the morning, and a feeling of being foggy-headed.

- Medications. Hair loss can also be a side effect of medications like beta-blockers, antidepressants, cholesterol medications, birth control pills, or even too much of certain vitamins like vitamin A.

- Genetics. Genetics determines a lot about your hair, including its shape, texture, and color as well as what's called female pattern baldness or androgenic alopecia, where hair is thin at the front and on top of the scalp. Though the other causes of thinning hair are often remedied when the underlying problem—like the nutritional deficiency or stress—goes away, genetic hair loss can be permanent. Talk to your doctor about possible remedies.

What other things can damage hair?

- Smoking. Each hair follicle needs nutrients and oxygen to grow and in order to get these things, good circulation is a must. As mentioned in the skin care chapter, smoking cuts off the supply of oxygen and as a result circulation to the hair. It's also believed that smokers have four times as many gray hairs as their nonsmoking counterparts and that smoking can cause thinning hair.

- Chlorine and salt water. Both can strip hair of natural moisture, making it dry and prone to breakage. (Chlorine can also give blonde hair a brassy, faded look.) Before getting in the pool or ocean, wet your hair with regular water, which fills in any porous areas, limiting the penetration of chlorine and salt water and their damaging effects, and wear a bathing cap. You can even go one step further and apply a thin layer of conditioner to wet hair before swimming so you hydrate it while keeping chlorine out. Shampoo and condition hair immediately after swimming (especially if you're staying outside since the sun's heat makes chlorine and sea salt more damaging) and if you're in the water several times a week, deep condition regularly.

- Heat styling. High heat can cause breakage, so make sure to use a blow-dryer, flat iron, or curling iron only when necessary, and apply heat protective products beforehand. When blow-drying, try to get hair at least 80 to 90 percent dry first and use flat or curling irons on dry hair only.

- Indoor environments. Both high heating and air-conditioning can draw moisture out of hair, leaving it dry and brittle. Apply moisturizing products like humectants and leave-in conditioners.

- Sun. UV rays can dry hair as well as strip and fade color. Luckily, there are many leave-in sprays and styling products that contain UV filters to shield hair from the sun's rays or for extended time outside, slip on a hat. (The sun can also cause skin cancer on the scalp so a hat or sunscreen on your part is a must.)

I'm confused by the different types of hair color and techniques. What do they all mean?

Hair color, which offers many opportunities to easily change your hair and add shine and dimension, is actually pretty simple when you break it down. First, color falls into three main categories.

- Permanent color, as the name implies, does not simply wash out of hair, but instead needs to grow out. Permanent color can make hair lighter and darker and cover grays.
- Demi-permanent color lasts up to twenty-four shampoos. It can make hair darker or brighter, but not lighter and can be used to blend a small amount of gray.
- Semi-permanent color lasts about eight shampoos. Because it's short-lived (it simply stains the surface of the hair), it's a great way to test-drive a color before making a long-term commitment. Semi-permanent color can be used to make hair darker or brighter and can cover a small amount of gray.

There are also three techniques for hair color.

- Highlighting and low lighting add strands of color throughout your hair and are a great way to blend gray hair so that it looks natural without the maintenance of all-over color. Highlights are created using a color that's lighter than your natural hue, while lowlights are created by using a color that's darker. How often you'll need touch-ups depends on how many shades you go away from your natural color, but it's about every eight to twelve weeks.

- All-over color is used to give hair an overall change of color, which can be lighter, darker, or brighter. Depending on whether you're covering gray, lightening or darkening your hair will determine how often you have to have it touched up, but the average is about four to eight weeks.

- Block coloring adds dimension into the hair by using three or more colors. Again, how often you need this touched up depends on how far away your block-coloring is from your natural color, but the average is four to six weeks.

I can't afford to color my hair at the salon. What are some at-home coloring tips?

- Stay within two shades of your natural hair color. For more drastic changes, seeing a professional will give the best results.

- Use the information on the package to determine which color is right for you. Often, they show you pictures of what your hair looks like now along with what it will look like after using that color.

- Call the 800 number on the box if you have any questions about which color to choose or the coloring process.

- At home, color a test strand that's half as wide as a finger (simply cut a small piece from underneath and in the back). Lay it down on a piece of white paper towel because the contrast with the paper gives you a true read of the final shade.

- If you're touching up your color, apply it only to the new growth at the scalp to minimize damage.

- Some brands like Clairol, have a Web site where you can upload a photo of yourself and see how various colors look on you.

- Make sure color is applied for the amount of time specified—too short may not penetrate well and too long may not give you the result indicated on the box or hair swatch.

- Don't save any unused color for future coloring. It's typically designed to be used within two hours; otherwise it may not be as potent or give the same results.

What should I consider before coloring my hair?

- What sort of look am I going for? Natural or bold?
- How often do I want to go to the salon to have it done or do it myself at home?
- What is my budget? How much do I have to invest in keeping my hair looking shiny and healthy? Knowing this up front will prevent you from getting into something you don't want or are unable to maintain.

7

What's Makeup Got to Do with It?

W hy don't you try these?" asked Tina, the show's makeup artist, as she handed me three tubes of lipstick. "They're the hottest colors right now."

I shook my head.

"*Robin*, you've been wearing that same color for years," she said. (Ten, to be exact.) "The camera really puffs up your lips, and that shade just makes them look bigger. Let's just *try* something lighter."

"But my lips *are* big."

Tina attempted her closing argument: "The all-natural look is really pretty."

"Nope," I said, shaking my head. Then Tina and I looked at each other and started laughing. Every few months, we have this same conversation, and every time it ends exactly the same way. (But I'll give her points for being persistent.)

Now, I think Tina is an absolutely brilliant makeup artist who does a phenomenal job on the show and photo shoots, and I'm certainly no makeup expert. But I *am* an expert in my own makeup thanks to decades of practice. Though I love experimenting with different looks, I know exactly what I like and when I find something that works (like Laura Mercier Lip Glacé) I stick with it.

> **Robin's Rx** You may love the look of lip gloss or plain old petroleum jelly, but its shine may attract the sun's UV rays and thus increase your risk of skin cancer. Instead, make sure your gloss contains sunscreen, or put a balm or lipstick that contains an SPF underneath your gloss.

Long before I was anywhere near a camera or Hollywood, I had a real passion for makeup—the result, I believe, of both my critical eye for design and creativity that I inherited from my mother and the fact that I had three older sisters. Growing up, all of them, especially the two eldest, were very girlie girls and with them around, "makeup" was practically one of my first words. That may be an exaggeration, but some of my earliest and favorite childhood memories are of my big sisters taking turns making me up. I loved it—especially in middle school when they'd cover my dreaded freckles—but my poor, sweet father felt otherwise. One of just two men in a house full of women, my father was very protective of his daughters and never wanted any of us to go out looking too done up or, though he never used this word, *trashy*. When we'd leave the house, he'd give our clothes, hair, and makeup a quick once-over and comment. I can still hear him saying things like, "You girls need to tone down that makeup" or "You need to flatten that hair" (admittedly, we *did* go a little nuts when the bouffant was in).

When my sisters weren't making me up, I was doing it myself. And just like I'll research doctors, menopause, and vitamins, I'll research cosmetic lines. Back in my twenties, I didn't have a lot of money to spend on makeup, and the quality of drugstore products wasn't close to what it is today— which is fabulous, so don't overlook drugstores and mass merchandisers when you need to stock up on cosmetics. In fact, nowadays several chain stores let you return opened makeup. This allows you to test products at home and not worry if you buy a color you don't like. (Just make sure to ask about the store's return policy before you buy.)

But back then, this wasn't an option, so to get a sense of what I liked and should invest in, I'd go to the different department store cosmetic counters like Clinique, Estée Lauder, and Prescriptives, among others, and let them show me how to use their products. This is something I really recommend because it's like a free makeup lesson. Most of the people working at those counters are highly trained, and many are quite talented. In fact, some of today's top celebrity makeup artists started their careers giving free department store makeovers.

So on my lunch hour or day off, I'd go up to one of the women working at the makeup counters and say, "I have half an hour and really want to learn how to do my eyes." While the makeup artist did my face, I'd watch in the mirror; but if that wasn't possible, I'd ask her to write down exactly what she used and why and where she put it and how. Of course, I also didn't hesitate to ask lots of questions along the way like, "Why are you doing X?" or "What did you put on top of Y?" I also realized that many of these talented artists could share some fascinating tips on how to use makeup not only to play up your best features but to play down your worst. For example, you can ask them, "How can I minimize my wide nose?" or "What can I do about my thin lips?"

Robin's Rx Often when I'd buy makeup at a department store and get those "gifts with purchase," about the only thing that I actually wound up using was the cosmetics case the products came in. The makeup was always pretty but rarely came in colors that worked for me—especially the lipsticks, which were always too dark. So when the boys were growing up and it was one of their birthdays, I'd use those lipstick samples to write "Happy Birthday!" on the bathroom mirror or their age on the shower door or toilet lid. I always loved starting their special days in a fun way, and they always loved waking up to that little surprise.

Unless I *knew* that I loved a particular item, I didn't buy the products right then and there. Instead, I'd go about my day wearing the makeup to see if I liked both the colors and product. Often, they'd give out little samples, which gave me a few days to see how my very sensitive skin reacted. If I liked the look and my skin didn't get inflamed or break out, I'd go back and buy a few things. But if I didn't like it, I'd also go back to the same counter or another one and try again. I'd say, "The last time you circled my lids with liner and it didn't work for me. Can you show me another way to make my eyes pop?" Sometimes I'd go when I knew we were going out to dinner or had a special occasion to attend. After all, why waste a good makeover? It may seem intimidating to go up to those counters at first (especially when you feel like you have to buy something, so just remember that you don't). Think of it as a fun, free way to be pampered and learn. After all, it's such a confidence boost when you know how to make yourself look your best. Something as simple as figuring out how to do that smoky eye you envy or how to cover a blemish can make you feel fabulous.

My lessons from department store makeup artists, coupled with lots of my own experimenting, made me an expert in applying my makeup and knowing what looks best on me, so much so that I actually do most of my own makeup for the show. (Although of course, Tina helps—but more on that in the pages to come.)

Robin's Way

I love experimenting with makeup and new products, but there are some products that have been staples in my cosmetic case for a while now that I simply can't go without.*

- Laura Mercier Lip Glace in various shades of pink
- Chanel Precision Lip Definer in Sienna
- La Prairie Cellular Treatment Rose Illusion Line Filler
- Clé de Peau Concealer
- Clé de Peau Silky Cream Foundation
- Clé de Peau Contour Defining Powder
- Shu Uemura Eyelash Curler
- Estée Lauder Lash Primer Plus
- Chanel Intense Volume and Curl Mascara in Smoky Marine
- Yves Saint Laurent Luxurious Mascara in Burgundy
- Maybelline Great Lash Mascara
- Max Factor Natural Cosmetic Sponges
- MAC Brush Cleanser

*I have no financial or commercial interest in any of the products, services, or professionals mentioned in this book.

On a day when we're taping, I shower, put on my facial moisturizer, and after that dries, apply a makeup primer. I've been wearing primer for years because I love how this first layer fills in any little lines or imperfections giving me a smoother, more even surface on which to apply my makeup. It also prevents makeup from settling into fine lines, which only makes them more noticeable. Though I've used various products, my current favorite is La Prairie Cellular Treatment Rose Illusion Line Filler because it glides on and hydrates skin, something that's important for mature complexions. While the primer dries, I make myself a cup of coffee.

Next, I pull out the concealer, something I've worn since my twenties and thirties when I struggled with acne and folliculitis. Because of these skin conditions, I've tried lots and lots of concealers and truly thought I'd found heaven when I discovered Clé de Peau Concealer. Available in three shades, I wear ivory, which is the lightest. It gives me amazing coverage but still feels light on my skin and stays put for hours (and that's especially important when we tape two or three shows in a row). It comes in a lipstick-like tube so I draw a thin layer on my face where I need it and then I smooth and blend it really well with a makeup sponge. But not just any old sponge. I know so many makeup artists who swear by those little, white triangle sponges, but they just don't seem to work for me. I think they absorb too much makeup and create friction, making it hard to move them around my face. Instead, I use Max Factor Natural Cosmetic Sponges that I discovered twenty years ago in a Safeway store in Wichita Falls, Texas. They're not easy to find anymore, so when I can, I buy them online and really stock up. I also love the pink, teardrop-shaped sponges by Beauty Blender that Tina found about a year ago. (They're available at beauty supply stores or online.) Both of those sponges blend so beautifully and smoothly that my skin looks creamy and flawless, not dry and cakey. They also help keep my makeup from getting into the tiny smile lines around my mouth. To me, blending your makeup is the key to making it look natural and not obvious, so I take that sponge and blend and pat it all around my lips, nose, and eyes until it's smooth.

On days when we're not taping the show and I'm just running errands or hanging around the house, all I add to that well-blended concealer is a little lipstick and I'm done. But if I'm in front of the camera, my next step is Clé De Peau Silky Cream Foundation in shades B10 and a bit of B20 that I mix on a plastic palette. I apply it from the bottom of my eye to my jawline and blend with those beloved makeup sponges. I follow this with powder, a product I know many people think you *shouldn't* wear as you get older. In my opinion, that's a beauty myth like the one about having to cut your hair short after a certain age, and I don't buy it. I've worn powder for decades because it gives my makeup a finished look and helps it stay put longer. I'm careful not to use too much (or else it can highlight some of your lines and wrinkles, making them more obvious) and blend it well all over my face patting it lightly with a powder puff. My current favorite powder is Clé de Peau Contour Defining Powder, which contains tiny, light-reflecting particles that give skin a smooth finish because they actually cause light to bounce off of them, blurring lines and blemishes and making them look less noticeable. It's sort of an optical illusion, but it works. Many cosmetic companies—from drugstore brands to department store lines—offer products like foundations, powders, and tinted moisturizers with these light-reflecting particles (also called optical diffusers) and they say so on their labels. I'd suggest giving them a try if you want to minimize the appearance of little lines, blemishes, or other small imperfections.

Next, I move on to my eyebrows. Experts are right when they say that the shape of your brows can give your whole face a lift and make you look younger. I agree, especially if you have droopy eyelids, since creating an arch gives the illusion of lifted lids, while having more skin showing at the brow bone opens the entire eye so you look more awake by drawing attention away from dark circles. That said, there is a fine line between showing enough skin in this area and tweezing brows too much. So even if you can't afford regular professional brow shapings, it may be worth it to have your brows done once by a professional at a spa or salon. This gives you a sense of the best shape for your face, and then you can often maintain it yourself by tweezing. Or treat yourself to one of the fabulous brow kits now available at places like Sephora and department stores. Many are created by top brow gurus (yes, there are actually people who specialize in brows) and contain all the tools—like brow stencils, powders, gels, and tweezers—and step-by-step instructions for creating your ideal arch.

I hate my eyebrows and always have (which is one reason I've had bangs for years now), but the issue is not the arch or length. In fact, my eyebrows grow so long that I have to trim them weekly. My problem is that they're too far apart. People have asked me why I tweeze them that way, but it's not me, it's just Mother Nature. That's how I was born and short of a brow transplant (which I'm not doing, though they do exist), there's not much you can do about that. To fix them a tiny bit, I use a dab of brow powder and a tiny brow brush to fill them in and shape them (always work in the direction that the hair grows) and then use a little clear brow gel to set them. I don't do very much of this because I don't like the fake brow look, but I do give them a little attention.

Following this, I work on my eyelids, an area I really have fun with. Standing in front of my mirror, I gently lift my brow up in order to create a flat surface to work on. (I started doing this in the last few years when I noticed that my lids were getting wrinklier.) First, I take a base color of eye shadow—usually something with a little gold in it—and using a shadow brush with flat, wide bristles, I cover from my brow to my lashes. (Start with the area closest to your nose and work toward the outside using a pressing motion.) This creates a really nice, smooth surface on which to layer my colored shadow and helps it last longer. Then I dip my shadow brush in a color like copper or plum (depending on my mood and what I'm wearing), tap it off on a tissue to get rid of excess product, and fill in the crease. I usually start at the outer corner of the eye and work inward along the crease, moving the brush back and forth in a windshield wiper motion.

Though I recently stopped wearing eyeliner because I thought it made me look too done up, I do run a black liner pencil along the underside of my upper eyelids a few times in order to make my lashes look thicker and pop more. Of course, I can't stress enough that you have to be *extremely* careful when putting a pointed pencil under your lids, so this isn't something to do when you're in a rush or driving. If I need to look more awake and alert, I'll line the bottom lid with a white pencil or—get this trick I learned from a makeup artist—the corner of my eyes with a light blue pencil.

After this I focus on my lashes, which is a great way to give your eyes definition. Now I have to say if I were heading to a deserted island and could only take a few things, my Shu Uemura Eyelash Curler would top my list (besides Phillip, of course). That's because my lashes go straight down so, despite their long length, it's hard to see them. Because of this I take that lash curler, place it as close to the lash line on my upper lid as I can, and pump it a few times to get a good curl. What I love about curled lashes is that they open your eyes, so they're ideal for making it look like you got a good night's sleep even when you're totally exhausted.

The second thing I can't live without is Estée Lauder Lash Primer Plus, which comes in a tube like mascara but goes on white and dries clear. Just a couple of coats really build up my lashes so I don't have to wear as much mascara and help it stay put. (It's also great on my lower lashes, which are so long that I can't wear a lot of mascara or it winds up on my face.) I follow this up with two kinds of mascara, though before I apply either of them I wipe the tips of the wands on the top of the mascara tube to remove any excess that can leave lashes looking clumpy. The first one I put on is Chanel Intense Volume and Curl Mascara in Smoky Marine, which is a blue mascara that's absolutely gorgeous. Don't ask me why I picked blue. There's no rhyme or reason; I just adore the way it looks. When that dries, I layer on mascara, either Yves Saint Laurent Luxurious Mascara in Burgundy, a rich color that really makes my eyes pop, or Maybelline Great Lash Mascara, an old favorite that I've been using for decades. I start corner to corner and coat my lashes about ten times. Then I take a little of the eye shadow that I used on my lids and with a tiny brush form a soft shadowing on the outer edge of my lower lashes. This draws attention away from the fact that my eyes sometimes come together.

At this point, almost twenty minutes have passed but I'm nearing the end. I take a big powder brush, dip it into my MAC blush (I use two shades Buff and Swoon), tap it on the bathroom cabinet to get rid of excess color and smile really big, applying the brush softly to the apples of my cheeks. I also run the brush close to my hairline above my brows and the corners of my face, blending it really well. The grand finale is lip color, something I've always worn because my natural lips are so pale (and tend to lose color as you age) that without it I look really washed out. I line my lips with Chanel Precision Lip Definer in Sienna smooth it out so it doesn't look so dark and end with a few swipes of one of the pink shades of Laura Mercier Lip Glacé.

Robin's Rx Did you know that there's often a quarter of an inch or more of lipstick left in the tube when you can no longer reach it? Save that leftover lip color by scooping it out and putting it in a small plastic palette or pillbox. Then just use a lip brush to apply it.

Finally I'm good to go and head to the studio. Once there, Tina takes a look at my makeup and does some touching up in order to make it camera ready.

Just like hair, the face looks different on TV so makeup that would be pretty for day to day may not be enough. In that case, Tina adds a little bit more to define my jawline or eyes and throughout the show she will come over and add powder to minimize any shine and lip gloss when it wears off. Tina always says she's amazed at how well I can apply my own makeup, but despite praise from such an expert, I was nervous when the show switched from standard definition cameras to high-definition (HD) at the start of the seventh season. Like most people, I prefer watching high-definition TV because the images come across in such amazing detail that you feel closer and part of the action. However, it's that attention to detail (and thus attention to every fine line, hair, and blemish) that makes those in front of the camera—myself included—panicked. I remember watching the first show that they shot with the new HD cameras. We had a female guest who would have looked fine if we used the standard definition cameras. But in high-definition, you could see every one of the fine soft hairs on her face, hairs that we all have and that you'd barely notice in person! After that, I was certain that high-definition TV would expose my amateur hand and, as a result, I'd have to get up earlier than I usually do to have a professional do all my makeup. So you can imagine how thrilled I was when my test shots showed that my makeup techniques, combined with Tina's expert touch-ups, were fine. (Yea! I could still sleep for that extra hour.)

In addition to my day-to-day makeup application (which I never realized was so involved until I actually sat down to write it out for this book), I have some other favorite tips:

Regularly replace your makeup. You know it's time to get new mascara when the top of the tube gets all junked up, but you also have to replace other makeup in order to ward off any skin or eye infections and to maintain the quality of the products. Here's the general rule of thumb: replace mascara every three to six months (anything that's used on the eyes can get contaminated by bacteria); liquid liner, foundation, and concealer after six months to a year; and lip and eye pencils, lipsticks, and glosses every year. And of course, no matter how long you've had it, get rid of any product that looks or smells funny because this could be a sign of bacterial contamination or a breakdown of preservatives.

Get egg on your face—literally. One of my favorite ways to give my skin a lift before a special event or whenever I need a pick-me-up is to apply raw, whipped egg white to my face until it is dry and tight and then rinse it off before putting on my makeup. In fact, when we're traveling, I often call ahead to the hotel and have them send up the egg white so it's ready when I arrive. I swear it tightens skin and makes it glow.

Invest in good makeup brushes. If there's one thing most makeup artists agree on, it's the fact that it's worth it to spend money on good brushes and tools. I remember hearing one top makeup artist say, "Brushes are like sports equipment: the better the equipment, the better your game." I agree because the cut and quality of the bristles actually make application faster and easier as well as more precise. Unfortunately, the applicators that often come with your makeup aren't always high quality or are too small to get the job done. That said it's only the natural bristle brushes (made of sable, squirrel, or pony hair, for example) that tend to be expensive and experts say you only need these for powder products—like blush, eye shadow, powder foundation, and loose or pressed powder—because they pick up the color better than synthetic bristles and deposit it on skin in a way that doesn't let it streak. You can use the less expensive synthetic brushes on creamy products like lipstick or cream blush, foundation, or concealer. The truth is, if you take good care of your brushes, they will last for many, many years. That brings me to my next tip.

Clean your brushes regularly. Once a week, I gather all my brushes—I use about five, which are Brushes by Karen—and soak the bristles in a bowl with MAC Brush Cleanser, which cleans and disinfects them. However, you don't have to buy a product made just to clean brushes. Instead, you can simply use a very small amount of shampoo (baby shampoo is a great option because it's so gentle). Just make sure to soak only the bristles, not the metal barrel, or you risk loosening the glue that holds the bristles together. Then, I rinse the bristles well, making sure there's no cleanser left in them, and lay them on a towel to air dry.

On the subject of brushes, here's another insider tip that I love. You can actually save money by buying your natural bristle makeup brushes at the art store. Yes, the art store! You can still get the same pony-, sable-, and goat-hair bristles—in all sizes—at a fraction of the price. (You just may have to trim the handles.) As I said earlier, makeup at drugstores and mass merchandisers has gotten so much better over the years, and some do sell wonderful natural bristle brushes. But if you're shopping with a budget, you may want to compare these to the art store brushes and see which ones best fit your needs.

Invest if you find a product you love. I know that many good products carry high price tags, but there are some like my foundation or my favorite hair styling cream that I use so little of each time that a jar or tube can last me almost a year. So if you really like a pricey product and don't use a lot of it, it may pay to splurge.

Makeup can be a gift. Before I could afford to buy makeup, I'd always ask for gift cards to my favorite department stores or drugstores when my birthday or holidays rolled around. I mentioned this in the skin care chapter—telling your family or friends what you want may seem strange, but it's a gift-giver's dream. They don't have to worry about finding the perfect present, and you can choose exactly what you want.

Research the right colors for your face. Easier said than done. I know because it took me years to settle on the right blush. There was a time when I went too dark or orangey (or simply wore too much makeup altogether), and today you'd be stunned if you saw how bright pink my blush is. The best way to find the right color in anything from blush to foundation to lipstick is to experiment, visit those makeup counters, or ask a friend with a good eye.

I know that the subject of makeup may seem superficial (pun intended). But I believe that it's more than skin deep. Yes, in a perfect world we would all be okay walking around with our blemishes or lines exposed, but that's simply not realistic. As someone who spent years suffering with acne and folliculitis on my face, I know the confidence boost you can get from making that one blemish a little less noticeable. In turn that confidence boost lifts your self-esteem and mood, and then this good feeling permeates and improves everything in your life from your relationships to your work to how you carry yourself through this world. In my opinion, that's not superficial at all.

Answers from the Expert

Matthew Vanleeuwen, celebrity makeup artist whose clients include Heidi Klum, Scarlett Johansson, Salma Hayek, Kate Beckinsale, and Mariska Hargitay.

How can I use my makeup to help me look younger?

- One of the best ways to give an immediate lift and youthful radiance to the face is to take the focus *away* from the mouth by making your eyes the most interesting part of your face. (This doesn't have to mean wearing a lot of eye makeup, but can be as simple as curling lashes and applying mascara.) Then, you want to neutralize the color of your lips by using a beige or nude lip color that is similar or slightly lighter than your natural lip color. This simple trick draws the eye up the face to the eyes and cheeks creating a youthful appearance. Oftentimes, overly bright or dark colors cause the eye to focus on the jaw which is a masculine part of the face. This simple trick will make sagging skin around the jawline look less noticeable and you'll be amazed how this makes your complexion glow!

- For drier skin or a complexion with a lot of discoloration or brown spots, a loose mineral powder may help make them less noticeable. Minerals provide a lot of coverage yet reflect light in a very youthful way and can give you a dewier appearance.

- Less is more. Don't try to hide fine lines and wrinkles by applying a lot of makeup; it will just make matters worse by emphasizing them.

- Don't try to cover up every single age spot. That can require a lot of makeup, so you'll simply be trading discoloration for a pile of makeup that makes the texture of your skin look unnatural. Instead, apply your foundation or tinted moisturizer, which will at least make them stand out less.

- Don't use a magnifying mirror to do your makeup. No one else looks at you that closely, so you don't have to either. Otherwise, you'll see every unreasonable imperfection and if you start applying makeup to flaws that only you can see, you'll wind up wearing a lot of it, which can actually draw attention to things like lines, wrinkles, and discolorations.

- Exfoliate skin regularly because the smoother it is, the more light refracts evenly giving it a youthful glow. It also allows makeup to go on more easily so it looks natural and can help diminish fine lines.

How can I keep my lipstick from bleeding?

- First, you want to try to eliminate or reduce the lines on and around lips that cause the problem to begin with. To do this, regularly use a lip cream or wrinkle product made for lips that contains ingredients like alpha-hydroxy or glycolic acids. These exfoliate, so not only will you be able to slow down the aging process, but with the technology in today's products, you may be able to wind back the clock.

- Apply a lip liner before your lipstick. Its waxy consistency can keep lipstick from traveling.

- Put a tiny dab of foundation on your fingers and pat onto lips. This fills in the creases on the mouth, preventing lipstick from getting into them and migrating.

Any tips for finding the right shade of foundation?

- The amount of melanin, or pigment, in our skin changes as we age and as a result so does our skin tone. That means that you probably can't wear the same shade of foundation when you're forty years old that you did when you were twenty years old.

- When shopping for foundation, try to match the color on the lower jawline or breastbone. Matching your product to these areas will give a truer color and an overall even tone to the face.

- Most people choose foundation that's too light, so don't be afraid to experiment with a color that's a little deeper.

- The best light to look at foundation in is light that's coming straight at you, but not with light that's coming from above. If you're in a store and can't find this kind of light, go to a window or outside to see how it looks in natural light.

- Foundation should never alter or add color to your skin—that's what blush and bronzers are for. It should just even out your skin tone.

- If you buy a color that's just a bit too dark, you can lighten it up by mixing it with a drop of moisturizer.

Are there any makeup tricks to give my thin lips a fuller look?

- Apply your lipstick and then take a lip liner and apply it lightly to the edges, blending inward.
- Placing a teeny, tiny dab of pearly white, pale white, or pale gold eye shadow on the upper edge of the upper lip (the area called the bow) before you apply your lip color can really help. This attracts light, which gives the appearance of the lip being pulled out a bit. To apply, dab one finger very lightly in the eye shadow, make a kiss with your lips, and then pat your finger on that upper edge of the bow of the lip going a tiny bit over it, but not much. You can also use a bit of super-white pearly lip gloss instead of eye shadow.
- Then, take a lip liner that's the same color as your lips (or close to it) and draw a line that's just a half inch long, dead center beneath the bottom lip.
- Most people think that the answer to thin lips is more lip liner or a lot of lip color, but that's just like saying, "Everyone, look at my small mouth!" Also, darker colors can make your lips appear even thinner and narrower. Instead, try to find a beige or nude lipstick, which will make lips look bigger.
- Putting a tiny bit of lip gloss smack in the center of your lips can also make them look a bit plumper.

How can I make my lipstick last longer?

- Stay away from oily, ultrashiny lipstick because the more shine that a product has the more easily it can the slip off lips.

- Gloss doesn't last as long as lipstick. But typically, stickier lip gloss tends to stay put longer than gloss with a smoother feel; however, sticky lips don't always feel that good.

- Choose lipsticks that are matte or demi-matte formulations. These are made with more powder and the more powder in a lip color, the longer it stays on.

- Try mineral lipsticks. Minerals have an ability to bond with the skin so they often have more staying power.

- Before applying lipstick, dab a tiny bit of foundation on the mouth. This gives the color a little base to cling to so it won't come off as easily. Pat the foundation on the outer edges moving in toward the center.

- Lip liner's waxy consistency also helps hold on to lip color. Use a lip liner that's either close to the shade of your lip or to the color that you're going to put on. But don't draw a sketch around the mouth. Instead, start at the corners and shade inward so the color fades away in the center.

My lips are always chapped, making my lip color look awful. What can I do about dry lips?

There are a few options for keeping your mouth flake-free.

- To remedy dryness: Put your lips together and give a little smile, which tightens the skin of the mouth a little bit. Then take a warm, damp washcloth and, using small circles, rub it very lightly over your lips. This will remove 90 percent of the dry skin and, as a result, help lipstick stay on longer and wear more evenly so you don't end the day with a ring around your mouth.

- To maintain a smooth mouth: every morning, when you're brushing your teeth, close your lips and give them a very gentle brushing too.

- To prevent dryness: Use one of the lip creams that contain alpha-hydroxy or glycolic acids. As mentioned earlier, these products nourish the skin in this area and exfoliate to get rid of dryness (while repairing fine lines). This is essential as you age.

I color my hair. Do I have to change the color of my brows too?

That depends. The general rule of thumb about hair color and brows is that brows should never match the hair, but be about two shades lighter, maybe three. A trick for finding the right color for your brows: choose the brightest highlight in your hair or a middle tone and use that. So, for example, if you color your hair so it's an ash blonde, making brows a lighter honey blonde would be beautiful.

What can I do about dark circles under my eyes?

There are two kinds of dark circles—those that are in an under-eye area that is flat and those that are in an under-eye area that is puffy. How you make them look less obvious is very different.

Problem: Flat dark circles

- Apply a dab of eye cream and let it absorb into skin. This can keep concealer from looking dry.
- One of the biggest mistakes women make when it comes to dark circles is using a concealer that's too light. Dark circles tend to be a blue-gray, so a too-light color is just going to make this area look grayer. Instead, choose one that's no more than half a shade lighter than your skin tone. If the under-eye area is very dark, choose a concealer that is half a shade lighter than your skin, but that is a little more peach toned, because the peach color corrects the dark-ness and can cancel it out.

- Take a flat, acrylic brush that's about the size of your pinky and place it in the crescent area, which is the line of demarcation where the nose meets that dark circle. Rest the brush very meticulously against that line and with a patting motion, apply concealer only in the dark circle. Don't wipe or brush or you'll remove the product you just put on. Just put in very small strokes until the product has disappeared into the dark circle. If you're skilled with makeup, you can use the outer edge of your pinky instead of the brush.

- Don't cover up the entire under-eye area—another mistake many women make. Usually the whole area isn't dark, so it doesn't look natural. Also, don't carry the concealer right up under the lower eyelid. Most people have a tiny bit of puffiness under there, so you'll just make it look puffier.

- Dark liner and mascara on your lower lashes can draw more attention down to dark circles. Instead, keep them bare and take attention away from the darkness by making your upper lid and lashes look beautiful. For example, curl your upper lashes. This gives the most incredible lift (and also helps keep mascara from going under the eye).

- To brighten the eye area and look more awake, take something that is a little iridescent, like a silver or pearly white eye shadow or highlight pencil, and dab it lightly on the inner V of your eye area near your nose. Bringing more light to the area wakes up the eyes tremendously.

Problem: Puffy dark circles

- Less is more when putting any makeup on puffiness. Too much product can highlight the under-eye area, and you don't want to highlight something that's already coming (or puffing) out.

- Rather than applying concealer, simply use a light veil of coverage with your foundation over it. Keep it simple and find other areas to highlight that make you feel good.

More important than trying to hide puffiness is to address *why* you're puffy with the following tips for preventing both dark circles and under-eye bags.

- Though both dark circles and puffiness can be genetic and get worse as you age, they can also be the result of not getting enough sleep. The notion of beauty sleep is no myth, so try to get at least eight hours (which will help with a lot more than just these under-eye ailments).
- When the skin under the eyes gets thinner as we age, it exposes the blue veins underneath it making this area look dark. Eye creams that contain ingredients that thicken skin and promote collagen production like retinoids, peptides, and hyaluronic acid can help.
- Some people also get dark spots under the eyes because of sun exposure. If that's you, make sure you use an eye cream that has sunscreen in it (a regular sunscreen can be too harsh for this delicate, sensitive skin so look for one made just for eyes).
- Dark circles and puffiness may be a sign of allergies. If you think that may be the reason for your under-eye ailments, talk to your doctor or health care provider.
- Don't rub eyes. This can dilate blood vessels beneath the skin, making this area look darker and stretch this delicate skin.
- Cut back on alcohol, which can dehydrate skin. When this happens not only are wrinkles more noticeable, but the blood vessels under the skin are even more visible.

- Sleep on your back with your head slightly elevated on a few pillows because it keeps fluids from settling around the eyes.

- Deflate puffiness by covering your eye area with tea bags that have been steeped in hot water and then cooled in the fridge for about twenty minutes. Keep them on for about ten minutes. The tannic acid in tea is believed to help reduce swelling, and anything cool helps reduce puffiness because it constricts the blood vessels. For this reason, cooled slices of cucumber or a wet washcloth placed in the freezer for a few minutes can also help.

- Another favorite trick is to use Tucks Hemorrhoid Pads. Keep them in the fridge and when needed, take one round pad, fold it in half and place *under* the eye for ten minutes (they stick right to the skin). The witch hazel they contain is an astringent which helps depuff the delicate eye area.

- Limit your sodium intake since too much can cause water retention especially around menstruation and switch to sea salt. Also, make sure to drink at least eight glasses of water throughout the day, since this helps reduce water retention.

Do I have to spend a lot of money on my makeup to get high-quality products?

Time was when department store and high-end cosmetics were definitely superior to those available at drugstore and mass merchandisers. But that's certainly not the case anymore. In fact, drugstore and inexpensive options are so much better than they've ever been, so don't be afraid to stroll the drugstore aisles or those of your favorite big box store. You may be surprised to find that some brands at these stores aren't exactly cheap, but they're certainly more affordable than high-end products (often because you're not paying for marketing and packaging). The other great thing about these mass brands of makeup is that many of them have finally gotten to the point where the color you see in the bottle is actually the color you see on your skin. With this and other technological advances, you can easily buy high-quality makeup products and look beautiful on a budget.

What do I do about a big pimple?

Despite what a lot of people think, covering a pimple is actually pretty simple. But you have to first remember one cardinal rule: never pop a pimple unless you're absolutely sure that it's ready. And even then, do it after a hot shower (the steam helps open the pores a bit) and be very gentle on the skin. Simply take two Q-tips or fingers covered in tissues and gently press either side of the pimple. If it doesn't pop instantly, leave it alone. Otherwise, you can make matters worse and cause a bigger pimple, scar, or infection. Most huge pimples are created by their owner because of this. If left alone, most blemishes come and go without being noticed. That being said, everyone needs to cover one now and then, so here's some advice:

- Have a different concealer for blemishes. Make sure it's a drier formula, which will adhere to the skin much longer. (Most concealers that come in a pot or pan tend to be drier; the liquid ones that come in a wand usually don't stay on long enough and lack the necessary coverage.) A cult favorite that's been deemed "magic" is Laura Mercier Secret Camouflage, which is dry and comes with two shades in each compact to mix and blend.
- It's also important to use a brush to apply your concealer. This way you will cover only the blemish as opposed to using your fingers, which tends to make you apply product to too large of an area.
- Remember, less is more. Cover the pimple completely, but don't pile makeup on unnecessarily.

My lashes have thinned as I've gotten older. Any foolproof mascara tips?

There are several ways to fatten up lashes that aren't as lush and long as they used to be.

- Today, there are amazing mascara formulas out there that can dramatically increase the length and width of even the meekest lashes. Take a stroll through the mascara aisle and test out a few of these new products.

- If you've tried that and are still unsatisfied, a bit of soft liner can enhance a thin lashline. A thin line of charcoal gray powdered eyeliner gently applied at the lash line will create a smoky base that, when black mascara is applied, will make thinner lashes seem more full.

- If that doesn't do the trick, you can put a coat of mascara on, then gently dust the lashes with a bit of loose powder (dust the underside only) and then apply one more coat of mascara. This will pump up and fatten the lashes.

- Lastly, if you feel like splurging, there are lash-nourishing products on the market that actually encourage the growth of these tiny hairs. Though they tend to be a bit expensive, they are very effective for some people.

Any makeup tricks for making teeth look whiter?

White teeth are truly a sign of youth, so brightening your smile is a quick way to look a bit younger. Teeth naturally get yellower and darker as you age because of the staining they accumulate over a lifetime of eating and drinking things like berries, soy sauce, red wine, coffee, and tea. Plus, over time, the hard outer layer of enamel wears off and the darker inner layer can show through.

It's a tried-and-true fact that blue-based lip colors can make the teeth look a bit whiter whereas warmer yellow- or orange-based colors tend to bring out more yellow in the teeth. That being said, if you're trying to make your teeth look whiter via a lipstick shade, perhaps it's time to whiten them. There are various teeth whitening systems out there that are effective and come at various price points so they can fit all budgets. You can look for white strips, pieces of thin plastic that come covered with a lightening agent, or whitening trays at the drugstore, or you can talk to your dentist about custom whitening trays or in-office lightening procedures.

8

What's Fashion
Got to Do with It?

C an I borrow that blazer?" Lorie whispered during ninth grade home-room. "For Saturday."

"This?" I said, looking down at the handmade jacket I was wearing. "Are you serious?"

"Yes," Lorie said. "And you can wear something of mine. Anything you want."

"Okay," I said shrugging my shoulders.

Lorie smiled. I, on the other hand, was so embarrassed that I wanted to crawl under my desk. We both had dates to the football game that weekend, and I was convinced that Lorie was offering free rein of her closet out of pity. She knew that my mother made all of my clothes and felt sorry for me.

After all, I wondered, why would someone with a store-bought wardrobe want to wear a jacket made of remnants? The answer, it turns out, was that it was beautiful and unique, something I didn't realize at the time.

Besides our underwear and socks, my mother sewed everything that my brother, sisters, and I wore (she even made my Barbie doll clothes complete with tiny snaps and buttons). Money was very tight so we never got to choose the material for these outfits; instead, my mother would regularly scour the remnant bin at the fabric store and purchase the best pieces that she could find. Then, she'd bring them home and sit hunched over her sewing machine in the corner of her bedroom, working into the wee hours of the night. She was extremely talented and could simply look through magazines, see what was in style, and make her own patterns. One time she made me a halter-style prom dress out of hot pink and purple remnants. (Longing for something store-bought, I didn't appreciate how cute it was; of course, I wish I had that dress now.) Another time she made my father a gorgeous suit that would hold its own against anything in stores today. But, as a child and even as a teenager, I didn't focus on the amazing work she did or the attention to detail. All I knew was that my homemade and hand-me-down clothes made me feel that I was less than the other kids. I didn't see my custom wardrobe as anything but a sign telling the world that I was poor.

Today, I see my mother's influence in the clothes that I choose and believe it's why I can easily tell what looks best on my body. After all, having my clothes tailor-made gave me a sense of how they should fit. For example, I know that my pants and jeans usually need to be fitted with a straight leg rather than baggy and though they can have a little flare, it can't be too much. Shorter blazers with one button that hit at the hip are more flattering with my short waist (otherwise I look like I'm wearing Phillip's coat). And I look better when my shirts are tucked into my skirt or pants rather than hanging out.

Since I know what I like and dislike, I prefer to pick out my own clothes for the show rather than have the stylists do it. I trust those women immensely, but I'm very clear on what looks good on me and want to be in control of what I wear. So the night before a taping, I'll sit with Phillip while he's preparing. Then about thirty minutes before we go to bed, I head upstairs to my closet to decide what I'll wear for the next day's show. (Besides a few items for an emergency wardrobe change, I don't keep my clothes at the studio.) Once I've picked my outfit, I pack everything from shoes to jewelry in a little, wheel-away suitcase. After my shower in the morning, I slip on a warm-up suit and Ugg boots, toss my suitcase in the car, and drive over to the studio. There I head to my dressing room. In case anything is wrinkled, I steam it with a steamer and then I get dressed and ready for the show.

It's pretty simple, but it wasn't always this way. When we moved from Dallas to California six years ago, I wasn't sure what to wear in front of the camera. Though I've always been interested in fashion and clear on my clothing preferences, being on TV was a bit intimidating. After all, I was going from a soccer mom who fixed lunches, cheered at games and drove car pool to being on camera in front of millions of TV viewers. I expected someone to tell me how to dress, but when no one did, I somehow decided that I was supposed to wear suits, both those with pants and skirts. So for most of the first two seasons of the show, I wore pretty but simple suits mostly in brown, black, and gray with the occasional pop of color. Then one night, I was getting my outfit organized for the next day's show and was holding yet another brown suit in my hands. Though it had clean lines and nice detail, I gave it a once-over and thought, *This is ridiculous. This isn't me. I'm someone who wears jeans every day.* With that, I put the brown suit back in my closet and pulled out my favorite pair of skinny-leg jeans, black leather boots, and a cute top. I wasn't sure how anyone at the show or viewers would react, but I knew that I had to do what felt comfortable and wear clothes that showed the real me.

Looking back, I'm not sure where I got the idea that pantsuits were the appropriate attire for a talk show host's wife, but I'm glad I came to my senses. I realized that you should never dress for anyone but yourself. Wear what *you* feel good in and what defines who you are. For example, I love black (just look at the book cover) and always have. But once I stopped wearing the pantsuits and started wearing lots of black, viewers were chatting about it on the message boards. (Yes, I do read them.) Some viewers loved it, while others said that I wore it too much. A few posts suggested that I favored black because the camera makes you look heavy. (That's not my main reason, but if it makes me look slim that's fine by me.) Truthfully, I was surprised that anyone even noticed, but nothing surprised me more than one query: "Does Robin wear so much black because she's Goth?" The answer to that is no. I simply love black and I always have. I think it's sleek and elegant alone, combined with white, or punched up with color.

Around the house, I prefer a simple, athletic style; so when I come home from a taping, I slip on a sweat suit (my favorites are by Juicy Couture) or drawstring pajama bottoms and a slim-fitting sweater (I love those by Izod). I also wear Phillip's sweat socks—something I've been doing for at least twenty years and that he finds cute. I've always favored this more casual style of dress even when we were living in Dallas, long before we moved to Los Angeles. Back then, I was like most busy stay-at-home moms who volunteer at their kids' schools, drive car pool, shuttle their children to practices and activities, and attend their games on top of running a household. I also regularly played tennis or exercised, so I was in tennis or workout clothes 90 percent of the time. Still, I always made sure those workout clothes were neat and flattering, not huge and sloppy, and I think that's an important distinction to make. I get lots of e-mails from women who say they spend all day in their sweats or who don't get dressed up because they don't work outside the home. These women often add that they hate the way they look, don't feel stylish, or still want to look good but don't know how. I think it's great to be comfortable, especially when you're chasing after young kids, constantly on the go, or working long hours, but you don't have to wear your husband's old sweatshirt to do that. Instead, buy yourself a great-fitting sweat suit with a coordinating top and bottom or simple yoga pants and a little matching jacket. Then all you need is a basic white tank or T-shirt underneath and, voilà, you look neat and put together. An old, baggy pair of sweats costs just as much as a pair that fits and flatters your body, and today, you can find inexpensive but adorable options at many mass merchandisers and department stores.

The other problem with those huge, old sweats goes beyond your appearance. It affects your self-esteem and your mind-set too. I remember that feeling from when Jay was born. I was so busy as a new mom that I barely had time to brush my teeth or go to the bathroom, much less change out of my pajamas. I lived like this for a few weeks when I realized that an act as simple as putting on a clean shirt and pants or just a fresh pair of pajamas could lift my mood. You don't have to go the whole nine yards with hair and makeup, but something as basic as this can do wonders for your confidence and spirit. It reminds you, once again, that you are a priority and sets a tone for the rest of the day.

Another comfortable option is jeans, a wardrobe staple that I absolutely love. I think every woman should have at least one really good pair of jeans that fits well. Then you can wear them with flats during the day or dress them up with heels at night. I've worn jeans all my life and I like all kinds. Years ago, Levi's and Lee jeans were practically the only game in town, but today the denim offerings are staggering. There are so many brands and styles that you're bound to find one that fits both your body and budget. Of course, all those options can be overwhelming, so I suggest that you devote one day or afternoon to jean shopping. My favorite brand is Paige jeans. They tend to be expensive at around \$145, but they make me look leaner and taller (and that's priceless!) and they sit higher on the hip than most. But I'm not exaggerating when I tell you that I tried on at least fifty pairs of jeans before I found them. That's why I suggest going to a store that has a variety of styles, bringing a giant stack of them into the dressing room and trying on every single pair because they all fit differently. It's amazing to me that I can put on one style of jeans and look like I gained ten pounds and another style and look like I've lost that much. (Shop alone if having a friend with you will make you feel rushed because this is going to take some time.)

Another important point: size doesn't matter because it can really vary by manufacturer and sometimes even by the style of the jean. For example, in one of my favorite brands I wear a size 29; in another I'm a 27. I know some women refuse to buy clothes if they're not a certain size or smaller, but like I've said before, numbers don't bother me. I don't mind buying a bigger size if I love the way something fits. I also suggest being open to trying on styles that may not seem like they're you. I've done that a few times and I've been surprised when these turn out to be something I love. I admit, finding the right pair of jeans does take work because you actually have to try them on and can't simply go by what looks good on a friend, in a magazine, or on the rack. But once you find the best pair for you, you'll see that it's all worth it.

Now, I know that my love of denim may break the unwritten rule about clothes that says that you shouldn't wear jeans after celebrating a certain birthday. But that's one rule I simply won't follow. I plan to wear jeans well into my sixties, seventies, and beyond. Still, around the time that I turned fifty, I wondered if I should start adhering to some of the other fashion rules for older women. For example, I decided that I was too old to wear shorts. After all, though my legs are toned, they're not as firm as they used to be and the skin's a bit wrinkled. So for about five summers, I banned shorts from my wardrobe until one day, it hit me: I thought, *Who cares? These are my legs and they're not going to be perfect.* In fact, I work hard enough at the gym so they're not going to look any better than they do today; I might as well show them off.

Robin's Way

I'm often self-conscious of my pale skin when I'm wearing an open or shoulder-baring top or dress, but I recently discovered a product that smoothes skin without looking thick or heavy. It's called Dior Skin Airflash Spray Foundation. Though it's made for your upper body, it can also make bare legs look flawless.

I realized that I had to accept the fact that my body is going to continue to age every day of my life—and it's going to happen whether I like it or not (and whether I wear shorts or not), so there's no reason to let it control me. The same thing happened with bathing suits. I never sit in the sun because of my fair skin and I'm not a big swimmer, so I hadn't worn a swimsuit in over a decade. In fact, I owned just one and it was buried deep within my closet. Then last July on our family vacation to Europe, I thought, *Why not wear a bathing suit?* I'm as fit as I'm going to be. I'd also heard that women my age should lower their hemlines and wear their skirts below their knees, another rule I considered. But I realized that no matter how old I am, a skirt that hits somewhere around my calves will just make my legs look stocky and thick. No, you won't find me wearing a mini anytime soon, but I'll still hem my dresses and skirts a few inches above the knee because it seems to elongate my body.

As you can tell, I love fashion and clothes (though I hate shopping, so go figure). But I get many e-mails from viewers who are confused about how to dress or think that they're too old to look good. I don't believe this for a second and think you can look hip and modern regardless of your age. I'm not saying that you should dress like a teenager or women who are decades younger than you are, but you don't have to look or feel dowdy just because you're older. I also get e-mails from women who say they only get dressed when they're going somewhere or don't deserve nice clothes because they don't work outside their homes. Again, I disagree. No matter what you do every day, whether it's at home or out in the world, you deserve to feel good in your clothes and like the way you look. Of course, I'm no fashion expert, but I have learned a few things over the years that really work for me.

You can't go wrong with classic items. I've always been a classic dresser, not someone who follows trends. Some of my favorite items—besides jeans— are sleeveless turtlenecks, white button-down shirts, slim-fitting boots, and simple, well-fitting blazers. One foolproof outfit that will make you look pulled together no matter where you're going is a crisp, white button-down shirt and jeans. (To me, a cute pair of heels is a fabulous final touch.) In fact, that's what I'm wearing on the cover of my last book though it wasn't intentional. I'd actually spent all day being photographed in at least five different outfits. When the shoot ended, I slipped on my jeans and white shirt and was about to head home when the photographer stopped me. "Let me photograph you in that," she said. I agreed, stepped onto an area with a white background and believe it or not, that was the photo that came out best!

Don't blindly follow trends. Yes, I like being current and modern in what I wear, but I won't buy something just because it's hot in the magazines. I always laugh when I read those articles that list one column of clothes that are "in" and another that's "out" because inevitably something I love winds up on the "out" list (often only to come back "in" the next year). Instead of following someone else's list, I choose my clothes on how they fit my body. Recently, for example, full baggy jeans were "in." They looked adorable in magazines, but I knew they'd just make me look like I'd put on a few pounds. Knee-length shorts were another trend that I walked right by (pun intended). Knowing my body and how clothes fit, I could see without trying them on that they'd cut my leg in a strange spot and be unflattering. Then again, sometimes I'll find a trend that looks great in magazines and have to give it my own little tweak to make it work for me. Recently, scarves were in all the stores, and I loved how they looked casual yet elegant in magazine photos. But when I tried on the exact scarf that I saw a celebrity wear so beautifully, it looked like I'd wrapped the comforter from my bed around my neck. In order to wear a scarf, I realized, I need a shorter, thinner version.

Robin's Rx Though big purses are in style, they're not always healthy for you. That's because we tend to fill them to the brim, and a too-heavy handbag can cause back, neck, and shoulder strain. Prevent this by carrying only your essentials in your purse and regularly alternating which shoulder or hand you use to carry your bag.

Also, check your children's backpacks to make sure they're not too heavy. Research shows that 19 percent of children miss at least one day of school or activities because of back pain from their too heavy backpacks and girls ages eleven to sixteen are at the highest risk. More than seven thousand children were injured in 2007 due to these overloaded bags, some weighing as much as forty-five pounds, says the U.S. Consumer Product Safety Commission. Experts recommend that backpacks weigh no more than 10 percent to 15 percent of a child's weight, but the average backpack weighs in at 20 percent.[1]

Comfort is key. No matter what you're wearing, think beyond how you'll look. Think about what you'll be doing and then test it out while trying on the potential outfit. I wish I'd heard that advice before the first red carpet event I went to almost seven years ago. It was the daytime Emmy Awards, and I had a beautiful green dress custom made for me. It looked great when I was standing in one place, but what I didn't think about was how snug the bodice would feel after sitting for hours. Another time we went to a charity ball and I wore a gorgeous black designer dress. Unfortunately, my chest was spilling out of the top so I spent the whole night pulling my dress up and feeling self-conscious. I couldn't believe that I was in this expensive gown and all I kept thinking was, *I hate this dress!* It was the worst feeling. Most of us have been there and made our fashion faux pas. Unfortunately, I have to look at those pictures over and over again. For some reason, when they write those made-up tabloid stories about Phillip and me getting a divorce, they seem to choose those pictures. (At times, I mind the pictures more than the lie that my marriage is crumbling!)

Robin's Rx A producer at work recently told me that she and her friends have regular clothes-swapping parties. I've never done it but think the idea is brilliant. You meet at one friend's house and each brings along any unwanted clothes that are in good shape and then swaps them with friends. We all make shopping mistakes and buy things that we love in the store but can't stand when we get home. This is a great way to salvage a shopping faux pas—and have some fun too.

You don't have to spend a fortune to look gorgeous. Though I love designer clothes, I also love that nowadays you can look stylish on a dime. There are so many inexpensive stores that offer high-fashion items without the high price tags. One of my favorite places to shop is Target because of the adorable and affordable clothes they have made by top designers. For example, I was recently on the *Rachael Ray* show and wore an outfit that was head to toe from Target. Everything including the earrings, belt, and shoes was just $120. The audience was shocked and so was I! Another time, I was excited to find a well-fitting and flattering pair of ten-dollar jeans that fit as well as some of the pricier pairs in my closet.

> **Robin's Rx** As I mentioned, I love my four- to six-inch heels. But after a long day of wearing them, my feet can feel tired and achy. Phillip rubs them for me, which really helps—though sometimes his big hands are too strong and I have to say, "Honey, remember I'm a girl." It feels fabulous, but another easy solution for sore soles is to take a tennis ball and rub it under your foot while sitting at your desk or watching television. It hits all the pressure points as it rolls along your soles, and you can vary the pressure by how hard you press down.

Accessories can instantly change an outfit or make something old look new again. I love accessories like a simple scarf, jewelry (my favorite new purchase was some inexpensive bangles), or purse and how they can really transform your look. But if I had to pick one accessory that's my weakness, it's shoes (though handbags are a close second). Maybe it goes back to my childhood when I always had just two pairs of shoes, a brown pair and a black pair, but for some reason I just can't resist. I've always preferred heels and it's not just because I'm five feet three inches and Phillip is six feet, but because I think they add elegance and a feminine touch to any outfit and make a woman look young, sexy, and tall. Mine are always at least four inches high, though usually six, and I swear that at least once a day I have someone say, "How can you walk in those heels?" My response: "I can run in them." (And I can!)

Shoe shop with care. To make sure your soles are as comfortable as possible, there are a few rules you should follow while shopping. Don't shoe shop in the morning. Feet tend to swell by the end of day (due to blood pooling in them), so afternoons are the best time to get a proper fit. Make sure to have your feet measured regularly, since things like weight gain and pregnancy can affect your shoe size. (In fact, my feet grew a half size with each pregnancy! I was a size 7 before I got pregnant with Jay and went to a size 7.5 after he was born and then after Jordan was born I went from a 7.5 to an 8.) And if one foot is bigger than the other—which is common for many people—buy your shoes to fit the larger foot. Also, don't assume that the shoe fits until you try it on (sizes vary by brand or even by style) and make sure to try shoes with the socks, pantyhose, or bare feet that you intend to wear them with. Lastly, no matter how much you love a pair of shoes, only buy them if they actually fit. I've heard stories of women cramming their feet into too-small stilettos or heels because they love them, but in my opinion, it's just not worth the pain. That said, shoes that are too big can cause blisters and calluses.

Don't be afraid to try new things. I love boots, but I always thought that I had to wear slim-fitting styles with my pants over them. Then I bought a pair of boots that turned out to be way too full around the calf. My daughter-in-law Erica urged me to tuck my jeans into them. "I'm too old for that," I told her. But she wore me down with her persistence, and not only did I try it, but I loved the way it looked. Now, I actually prefer it that way because somehow it makes my legs look so much longer.

Alterations can make all the difference. I've met many fashion stylists and designers over the years, and many of them have explained how just a few small alterations can make an inexpensive outfit look like it was made for you. Just having jacket sleeves shortened a few inches or tailoring your pants can make a big difference in how you look. And alterations don't have to cost a lot. In fact, some stores do them free of charge with a purchase, so make sure to ask.

Slim your silhouette with one color. And that color doesn't have to be black. Going monochromatic can make you look slimmer, so if you're wearing a skirt or pants and a top (as opposed to a dress), choose one color and don't break it up with a different colored belt. This creates one long line that elongates your body, making you look leaner.

Go below the surface. And I mean that literally. When it comes to fashion, what you wear underneath your clothes can have a huge impact on how your clothes look and fit. Believe it or not, 70 percent of women are wearing the wrong bra size. Perhaps that's because most of us figure out our size when we're buying our first bra and stick with that the rest of our lives. But our bodies change over the years, and things like weight gain or loss, pregnancy, breast feeding, and even just aging can change the size and shape of your breasts. The good news is that today getting fitted for a bra is easy. Many department stores have bra fit experts in their lingerie departments or host special fit events, as do specialty stores like Victoria's Secret. And even if your size does stay the same over the years, bras don't last forever. Over time the elastic stretches, fabric thins, and underwire loses its shape. As a result, your bras aren't giving you the lift and smooth lines that will make you look better. And an ill-fitting bra can cause back, shoulder, and neck pain. If you haven't been bra shopping in a while, you'll be intrigued by the technical strides that bras have made. Today, there are bras that minimize, maximize, and do everything else in between. They're made of unique fabrics that are comfortable, supportive, and seamless.

Robin's Rx You can't always find a professional to help you shop for bras, so here are some tips from Bali, the bra manufacturer.

- To figure out your size, use a tape measure and take a snug measurement under your breasts. Add five inches to get your band size. (If the result is an odd number, round up.)
- For the cup size, measure over the fullest part of your breast. Compare this number to your band size. If it's the same, you're a AA cup; one inch bigger you're an A cup, two inches bigger you're a B cup, three inches bigger you're a C cup, four inches bigger you're a D cup, and so on.
- Try before you buy; you can't tell if a bra fits without actually slipping it on.
- When trying it on, raise your arms above your head, reach your arms forward, and walk around a bit. This helps you see if the bra fits and is comfortable.
- If the bra cups are baggy, wrinkled, and not filled out, you probably need a smaller size.
- If your breasts are spilling out of the bra, either on the top or under the arms, look for a larger size and possibly fuller cups that provide more coverage.
- Try your shirt on over your bra to see how your clothes look with it on. And if you're looking for a bra for a special occasion dress, bring it with you to try on.
- Wearing a bra on the middle hook gives you the best fit.

While you're in the lingerie department, you may want to take a look at a new breed of undergarments called body shapers or shapewear. Unlike the girdles that your grandmother used to wear, these help smooth your stomach, butt, or thighs and can even give your butt shape and lift. They do so using comfortable, lightweight fabrics and come in a variety of styles, including stomach-smoothing high-waist panties and tank tops, thigh slimming shorts, and bodysuits that target an array of body parts, to name just a few. Often they're made without seams and include strategically placed control panels so they smooth bumps and bulges.

As I mentioned in the hair and makeup chapters, the clothes you wear do more than cover up your body. They affect your self-esteem and your confidence and make you feel like you're worth taking care of. You don't have to spend a lot of time or money on your clothes. Surprisingly, just having a few comfortable, clean items in your closet that highlight your assets and minimize your trouble spots can go a long way. The bottom line, in my opinion, is that you'll be amazed at how comfortable you feel in your own skin when you feel comfortable in your clothes.

Answers from the Expert

Cojo, fashion guru and author of the *Red Carpet Diaries: Confessions of a Glamour Boy* and *Glamour, Interrupted: How I Became the Best Dressed Patient in Hollywood.*

What are some quick and simple ways to look put together?

- Throw on a blazer, and you'll immediately look put together and stylish no matter what else you're wearing. Blazers are a classic item that come in an array of fabrics, but if you can only buy one, look for a jacket made of gabardine wool. It's a timeless fabric that you can wear year-round with pants, jeans, dresses, and skirts. Once you have that beautiful blazer, you can scrimp on the items that you wear underneath it like T-shirts, camisoles, and sweaters.

- If you're not the blazer type, try a shawl, long cardigan, sweater coat, or shrug. A T-shirt and jeans can be flat, but add a patterned shawl or long cardigan and you're instantly dressed.

- Trade sneakers for flats. It's all too tempting always to put on sneakers, but a pair of cute flats immediately adds polish to any outfit. Today, there are several inexpensive retailers that offer comfortable styles with designer details.

- Tie on a scarf. Even a plain shirt looks more refined when you slip a scarf around your neck and secure it with a simple knot. Or do what the women in Paris do and tie a scarf onto the handle of your handbag.

- Find fabulous costume jewelry. Timeless pieces are always pretty, like a gold cuff, gold bangle, or simple rhinestone bracelets. Another no-brainer way to look elegant is with a big pair of faux diamond earrings. They perk up your entire face and add sparkle to whatever you're wearing.

- Stock up on sweaters in universally flattering colors like pinks, burgundies, and blues. Though you can invest in gorgeous cashmere, you can also find elegant options in less expensive wool and cotton blends.

- Slip on a twinset. These matching cardigans and shells are available at every price point, fabric, and color imaginable. You can dress them up for work or a night out and down for car pool or a weekend barbecue. Wear them together or as separates and you can't go wrong.

- Forget about the little black dress. Instead, get a good quality dress with clean lines in a jewel tone like deep blue, magenta, a navy midnight blue, or deep burgundy. Or choose emerald green, which is flattering on most women. Like black, these colors are elegant, fashionable, and versatile, but they're a bit more modern.

- You can never go wrong with a clean, white button-down shirt whether it's yours or your husband's.

- Banish panty lines by wearing a thong. For clingy dresses, skirts, or pants, a thong will make all the difference in the world. It can smooth your hip line and backside and banish any underwear-induced bulges, making you look trimmer. And if you find the right pair, they're actually comfortable.

I'm a stay-at-home mom who's going back to work. But after years in jeans and sweats, I haven't a clue what to wear.

The best way to build a wardrobe is to start with just a few pieces.

- Instead of the power suit (where the top and bottom match), you can look stylish and up-to-date with separates. Try mixing a skirt in a fun print or plaid with a black blazer (or vice versa).

- Buy other skirts, pants, and blazers in black, white, and gray, which can easily be mixed and matched, and choose wool gabardine fabric, since it can be worn for all seasons.

- Add a white silky blouse and twinset to wear under blazers or alone.

- Find a simple, sleeveless shell dress that's closed at the neck. This basic item can be transformed with a blazer or cardigan or by adding a scarf or necklace.

- Give your outfit a modern bit of detail with accessories like a little gold chain, a pin, or dark red pumps.

How can I dress my age while still looking hip and stylish?

- Don't try to look younger. It just makes you look older.
- Remember this commandment from Coco Chanel and Audrey Hepburn: less is more. This is true for all women but is especially important as you age.
- Dark, tailored jeans are hip yet perfect for an older woman; let the teenagers wear the faded denim.
- Go light on showing skin, and no matter how toned your abs are, don't show your midriff.
- Wear clothes that fit the body, but never go skintight.
- Pick and choose which parts of a youthful look you're going to wear. For example, a woman in her twenties may wear a bohemian scarf and giant sunglasses with a ripped miniskirt. Pick one element (not the mini) like the scarf and make it your own.

What should I be looking for when I go into a store?

Shopping can easily be overwhelming because there are so many options out there. To make the best decisions, it's a good idea to make two shopping trips. The first is a no-pressure, casual visit to a variety of stores. This gives you a feel for what's in style and even a sense of what you like and don't like. (Bring a notebook or camera if you want to remember what you've seen and where.) Then go home, take a look at your clothes, and make a list of what you want to buy. On your second trip, you can start trying things on and talking to the salesperson about what you're looking for. This two-step process can help you avoid buying items that you'll later regret. If you're looking for something specific to go with an item you already own, take it with you while you shop. Also, bring along items that you tend to wear with the clothes you're in the market to buy. For example, if you're looking for jeans and always wear them with heels, wear or bring a pair along.

I want clothes that help improve my trouble spots. What can I do?

- Whittle your middle: Baggy, loose clothes may seem like the ideal way to hide a big middle, but they actually just make your stomach seem bigger. Make sure all clothes—be it sweaters, shirts, or coats—are more tailored and fitted rather than loose and boxy. Also, be careful with empire waist tops, which can make you look pregnant. Sturdy, rather than clingy fabrics can disguise less-than-six-pack abs. Ruched tops, which are those made of gathered fabrics, also help deflect from a full tummy as will a blazer left unbuttoned with a camisole or T-shirt underneath. Make that blazer black, and it'll take ten pounds off your appearance. Also, try drawing attention away from a large midsection by making your best assets look fabulous. If you got great arms, wear sleeveless tops and dresses; if you've got great legs, wear a skirt and colorful shoes that show them off.

- Conceal flabby upper arms: Skip the cap sleeve or sleeveless tops, which simply highlight your trouble area. Instead, choose three-quarter-length sleeves, which not only conceal fleshy triceps but also cut the arm at exactly the right place making it look longer. Bell sleeves also cover upper arms as well as draw attention down the arm. Or wear a button-down shirt with the sleeves rolled up just above the wrist.

- Minimize a large behind or pear-shaped lower body: Dark jeans in a boot cut look best because the slight flair balances out a larger bottom. Look for big pockets with stitching on them to make your derriere look more proportioned (rather than small pockets that just draw attention to your size). If you want to make full thighs look slimmer, avoid pants with cargo-style pockets in the front. Choose fabric made with a little stretch, but make sure pants aren't too tight. Again, wearing a blazer that hits below the hip can also help balance out a pear-shaped figure. When it comes to dresses and skirts, A-line styles help hide a full lower body. You can also balance out your proportions by wearing something that brings attention to your upper body like tops in light colors or fun prints or a loose top that hits at your hips (as opposed to a fitted top that hits at your waist). Heels can also help make your legs look longer.

- Distract from thick calves: Stay away from skintight leather boots, which bring attention to the area, and ankle boots, which cut your leg in a strange spot making them look chunkier. Instead, choose a pump (open or closed toe) in attractive colors like red or dark blues. Dark hose or long leggings are another way to slim your calves.

- Reduce the look of a large bustline: A minimizer bra can provide support and make a big bust look smaller. Also, choose tops that elongate your neck, like V-neck or scoop-neck styles (as long as they're not too low) or a blouse that's left a little open at the top. This takes attention upward and away from your breasts. Avoid high necklines, closed-neck tops like turtlenecks, and shirts with lots of ruffles, ruching or puffed sleeves, which can make the bust look bigger. Avoid those with pockets, embellishments, and stitching around the chest area, which draw attention to what you're trying to downplay. If your waist is slim, emphasize it with a belt or sweater with a banded bottom.

- Boy-shaped body: Create the illusion of an hourglass figure with slim-fitting, tailored tops and blazers that nip in at the waist. Dresses or tops with ruched waists or belts and wrap dresses also help define your waistline. Skirts that have pleats or layers can give your lower body some shape as opposed to straight styles like pencil skirts, which highlight your lack of curves.

- Clothes that cover any body part you're less than pleased with should skim the body, but never be too tight or too loose. Lastly, make sure to accentuate the positive. Rather than focus too much on the body parts you don't like, highlight your best features.

I'm petite. What are some tips for looking stylish and sexy?

- Hem skirts and dresses above the knee, which makes legs look longer. (Whereas hems that hit below the knee can give legs a stocky appearance.)
- Go monochromatic. Wearing one color elongates the look of your body.
- Don't let your accessories take over. Avoid huge necklaces, earrings, handbags, or even shoes that can overwhelm your small size.
- Make sure details like buttons, embellishments, and labels are in proportion to your body.
- Give yourself a lift with high heels or platforms. They tend to make legs look longer and slimmer especially those in a nude hue.
- Slim-fitting, tailored clothes are more flattering on your small frame than those that are loose and shapeless.
- Research clothes that are made just for you. Many designers actually have petite lines and many stores have petite sections. Often the proportion of these clothes results in a better fit.

Help! I have no idea what looks good on me. What can I do?

This is no easy feat, so ask a trusted friend, relative, or coworker who has a good sense of style to either come shopping with you or give you some tips on what you're doing right and what you could improve upon. (It's likely that they'll be flattered that you admire their fashion sense, so they'll be glad to help.) You can also talk to salespeople in the stores. You're not obligated to buy anything just because you ask for their help, but they know the inventory so if there's something that will work for you or that you're looking for, they can find it. In the end, you may develop a relationship with a salesperson who will keep you posted about new arrivals and upcoming sales and when an item you've been eyeing has been marked down.

I want to clean my closet. Where do I start?

Editing your closet is a tough but necessary task. It will help you feel less cluttered and overwhelmed because you can't find anything in your closet. Here are some tips:

- Toss anything from a former era. Don't wait for it to come around again; it won't.
- Keep—but don't wear—a few extremely sentimental items. But just a few. Store them carefully with tissue paper in a specific area. (If your closet is small, it may be in another room.)
- Have a friend or your teenage daughter help out. Another person can be more objective and tell you to toss items that are unflattering, out of style, or simply ridiculous. Plus, with another person you'll have more fun.
- Make piles: one of clothes to keep, one to throw out, and one for charity. The charity pile makes you feel better about letting go of certain items because they're going to others in need.

9

What's Faith Got to Do with It?

Throughout this book, I have talked about how I care for myself physically and emotionally. But I also work hard to maintain and care for myself spiritually. My mother raised my brother and sisters and me in a God-centered home, and her Christian faith was something that has inspired me so deeply. It was my mother who took me to church. It was my mother who taught me to read and study the Bible. And it was my mother who taught me about accepting Jesus Christ as my personal Savior.

My mother would always say that it would be up to me and only me to decide when the time was right. I wasn't sure what she meant. *How* would I know? Would Jesus call me on the phone? Tap me on my shoulder? I was confused. That was until one day when I was nine years old and visiting my mother's mother, Granny Lela, in Garber, Oklahoma. We were inside the beautiful, old, country church that she belonged to and I was sitting there daydreaming about the food that everyone had brought to eat afterward. (Yes, I think about food a lot.) Then, all of a sudden the preacher said, "If you want to accept Jesus Christ as your personal Savior, the time is now." And that's when I heard this little voice in my ear. That was my moment. A moment that changed my life forever.

Ever since that day, my relationship with the Lord has been so important to me. When my boys were young and living at home, I'd wake up in the morning and before getting out of bed, I'd thank God for all that he had blessed me with. I would also pray for him to watch over and protect my boys and husband. I always felt a close relationship to God and cherished that relationship deeply. But now that my kids are grown and I'm an empty nester, I have even more time to focus on him and to really enjoy my time in prayer. I never pray in just one place, but instead walk around my home and choose different rooms to sit in and feel God's presence. Then, I close my eyes, take a deep breath, and imagine myself as a small child climbing up on his lap, and I almost feel him hold me in his arms. It's like he is sitting there in all his glory and I am in his presence. My mother taught me to start praying that way as a young girl, and I've been doing it ever since because having that vision in my head makes me feel so close to him and so protected.

As I mentioned earlier in the book, almost every night while relaxing in the bath, I thank God for his love and guidance. But when I can, I also try to sit down for a one-on-one conversation with him. Doing this every day is not realistic for me, but even then I know that he is always with me, protecting me and guiding me. I feel his presence all around me. Then when the moment is right, I sit down, take my time with him, and really reflect. I do this at moments in my life when I'm troubled and at moments when I'm happy. It's a treat that I give myself. And when life gets in the way and I've been really busy and haven't taken that time with him, I know it. I get this feeling inside that is like no other and then I make it a priority to spend some quality time in prayer.

My faith has gotten me through many rough patches in my life because I truly believe that God has a plan for each and every one of us. And I believe that we should honor that plan. In fact, this belief is one reason why I think that I am so accepting of my age. I know that each year, each day, and each moment is a gift from God. I honor the path in my life that God has put me on and know that it is a privilege to be alive and to wake up and have another day with my husband and children. I am aware of that and I don't take it for granted.

At the age of fifty-five, I am just three years shy of the age that my mother was when she died. Even twenty-four years later, I feel sorry for all she missed out on, not only the beauty and joy that can be found in the nuances of daily life, but some major events in my life like the birth of my son Jordan (born one year to the day after she died), Jay getting married and his lovely wife, Erica, becoming a part of our family, and the publishing of my first book and now my second. She was an amazing and precious woman who really did love life and it brings tears to my eyes to imagine how much she'd love it even more today.

Still, I know that I can choose to dwell on the fact that my mother is not here and did not take care of herself, or I can realize that this was part of God's plan for her and for me. I choose to do the latter. I know that God has blessed me with the intelligence to realize how to turn that tragedy into something positive and that is what I hope I have done with this book. I hope you are inspired to take care of yourself so that you are there for your loved ones and for yourself, so that you can hold your future children or grandchildren, dance at their weddings, and see the kind of wonderful people they will grow into.

I said in *Inside My Heart* that women are the heart of the home, and that is something I truly believe no matter who you are or where you live. No matter if you're a stay-at-home mom or a mother working two jobs, whether you live in a small studio apartment or a sprawling house. When our children have a bad dream in the middle of the night, they automatically scream, "Mom!" even though they're still half-asleep. And when they come home from school after a bad day or skin their knees, it's our laps that they want to crawl into. Even when they're too big to sit in our laps, it's our embrace that makes them feel safe, secure, and protected. My hope is that you take care of yourself so that you can always be your family's soft place to fall. And even if you're not a wife or mother, my hope is that you take care of yourself so that you are around for the friends and loved ones who want and need you in their lives.

Earlier, I discussed the makeovers that we've done on the show and how they always start out as something I'm doing to make a difference in other women's lives, yet they turn out to make a difference in mine. The same thing happened to me while writing this book. I set out putting pen to paper (or fingers to keyboard to be more exact) in order to share my story and the advice of experts to inspire other women to learn to take the best care of themselves possible. And yet, after months of writing, I realized that something that started as a gift for other women has become a gift for me. It has transformed my life. I have learned even more about myself than I thought possible and gained insight into the woman I will be in my sixties, seventies, and beyond.

I believe that no matter how old we are, we women have the ability to be the healthiest, most energetic and vibrant individuals that we can possibly be. It just takes a little effort. One of my role models for this is Phillip's mother, whom we lovingly call Grandma Jerry. She is an amazing, adorable, and precious woman and at eighty-three years young, she still lives by herself, drives all over town, and has a very rich and full life that includes a great church and fabulous friends. I remember when Phillip's father died fourteen years ago and we all worried that after fifty-four years as part of a couple, she would wither away now that she was on her own. Yet, despite the loss of her husband, she not only emerged feeling okay, but carved out a new life for herself. It didn't make her miss her husband any less, but she was not going to let one of life's curveballs knock her down. She revealed her strength again eight years ago when she was diagnosed with lung and liver cancer. She went through treatment and today, she has been cancer free for five years. Her strength, passion for life, and vitality continue to amaze me and when I'm in my eighties I plan to be just like her, loving my life and appreciating and enjoying each new day.

Of course, I have a few decades before I reach my eighties, but I know that I am going to continue taking care of myself until I get there. I know that there is nothing selfish about deciding to become an active manager and nurturer of what God has given me. I'm going to continue to live my life with purpose and passion, always looking for ways to be healthier and always feeling proud of being a woman. And I truly hope that you do too.

Notes

Chapter 2

1. Maruit SS, Willett WC, Feskanich D, Rosner B, Colditz GA. A pro-spective study of age-specific physical activity and premenopausal breast cancer. *Journal of the National Cancer Institute.* May 13, 2008

2. Johns Hopkins Medicine Health Alerts, www.johnshopkinshealth alerts.com/reports/nutrition_weight_control/1811-1.html?type=pf

3. Robert Reames, *Makeover Your Metabolism* (Meredith Books; 2006)

4. Richard S Rivlin Keeping the young-elderly healthy: is it too late to improve our health through nutrition? Am. J. Clinical Nutrition, Nov 2007; 86: 1572S - 1576S.

5. Brian L. Sprague, Amy Trentham-Dietz, Polly A. Newcomb, Linda Titus-Ernstoff, John M. Hampton and Kathleen M. Egan Lifetime

Recreational and Occupational Physical Activity and Risk of *In situ* and Invasive Breast Cancer *Cancer Epidemiology Biomarkers & Prevention*, February 1, 2007, 16, 236-243,

6. Center for Disease Control, www.cdc.gov/nccdphp/dnpa/physical/measuring/perceived_exertion.htm

Chapter 3

1. National Osteoporosis Foundation, www.nof.org

2. National Osteoporosis Foundation, www.nof.org

3. Jack F. Hollis, Christina M. Gullion, Victor J. Stevens, Phillip J. Brantley, Lawrence J. Appel, Jamy D. Ard, Catherine M. Champagne, Arlene Dalcin, Thomas P. Erlinger, Kristine Funk, Daniel Laferriere, Pao-Hwa Lin, Catherine M. Loria, Carmen Samuel-Hodge, William M. Vollmer, Laura P. Svetkey, Weight Loss Maintenance Trial Research Group "Weight Loss During the Intensive Intervention Phase of the Weight-Loss Maintenance Trial," *American Journal of Preventive Medicine,* August 2008, 118-126

4. Alexopoulos N, Vlachopoulos C, Aznaouridis K, et al. The acute effect of green tea consumption on endothelial function in healthy individuals. *European Journal of Cardiovascular Prevention and Rehabilitation* 2008; 15: 300-305.

5. Tucker, KL, Morita, K, Qiao N, Hannan MT, Cupples A, Kiel DP. *American Journal of Clinical Nutrition.* (October) 2006; 84(4). "Colas, but not other carbonated beverages, are associated with low bone mineral density in older women: The Framingham Osteoporosis Study."

6. Sharon P. Fowler, Ken Williams, Roy G. Resendez, Kelly J. Hunt, Helen P. Hazuda and Michael Stern. "Fueling the Obesity Epidemic? Artificially Sweetened Beverage use and Long-Term Weight Gain" *Obesity* 16, (05 Jun 2008): 1894–1900

7. Phillip C. McGraw, *The Ultimate Weight Solution Food Guide* (New York: Pocket Books, 2004). Used by permission of Free Press, a division of Simon & Schuster.

Chapter 4

1. American Academy of Dermatology, www.aad.org/media/back ground/news/_doc/MinimallyInvasiveSkinRejuvenation.htm.

2. The Skin Cancer Foundation, http://www.skincancer.org/content/view/317/78/

3. The Skin Cancer Foundation, http://www.skincancer.org/content/view/317/78/

4. Whitmore SE, Morison, WL, Potten CS, Chadwick C. Tanning salon exposure and molecular alterations. *Journal of the American Academy of Dermatology,* 2001;44:775-80.

5. Koh JS et al. "Cigarette smoking associated with premature facial wrinkling: image analysis of facial skin replicas." *International Journal of Dermatology,* 2002 Jan;41(1)21-27.

6. American Academy of Dermatology, www.aad.org/media/back-ground/news/cosmetic_2007_08_02_newtechnologies.html

7. The Skin Cancer Foundation, www.skincancer.org/content/view/17/3/1/1/

Chapter 5

1. Mayo Clinic, mayoclinic.com/health/perimenopause/DS00554/DSECTION=symptoms; http://mayoclinic.com/health/hot-flashes/HQ01409

2. Mora S, et al "Physical Activity and Reduced Risk of Cardiovascular Events. Potential Mediating Mechanisms" *Circulation* 2007: 116:

3. Joanne M. Murabito, MD, ScM; Michael J. Pencina, PhD; Byung-Ho Nam, PhD; Ralph B. D'Agostino, Sr, PhD; Thomas J. Wang, MD; Donald Lloyd-Jones, MD, ScM; Peter W. F. Wilson, MD; Christopher J. O'Donnell, MD, MPH Sibling Cardiovascular Disease as a Risk Factor for Cardiovascular Disease in Middle-aged Adults, *Journal of the American Medical Association* 2005;294:3117-3123

Chapter 8

1. Washington University in St. Louis http://www.newswise.com/articles/view/542083/

Robin McGraw's
Complete Makeover Guide

Contents

How to Use
This Makeover Guide

W hatever your age, you and I have something in common: we're women, we're busy, and we want to look and feel our best, no matter how many birthdays we've had.

That's what this book is about.

Robin McGraw's Makeover Guide is designed to be a companion to *What's Age Got to Do with It?*

Each chapter in this workbook begins with a specific reading assignment from *What's Age Got to Do with It?* A Q&A section containing questions from readers like you will provide answers about beauty, health, fitness, fashion, and aging—all based on solid research and personal experience. I have also included some tips, lists, and other information to help you customize your own optimal health-and-beauty plan. Finally, a homework section will provide hands-on opportunities to take charge of your own aging process.

To get the most out of this workbook, you will need to purchase a journal so you can document your glamour and wellness decisions along the way. You will be instructed frequently to write down your questions, research, and plans, so don't start this workbook without a journal!

Now, if you're ready, let's get started!

1

What's Age
Got to Do with It?

READING ASSIGNMENT

Chapter 1 from *What's Age Got to Do with It?*

Q: How can I stop the effects of aging?

A: Here's the bare fact: you will age. From the moment we are born, we are already aging, and aging can never be stopped. But the good news is, the effects of aging can be minimized and, in some cases, reversed. The physical signs of aging can be reduced by making wise lifestyle choices with your nutrition, sleep, beauty, and more.

Let's look at some of the things that add the appearance of age and zap years from our lives:

Things That Age Our Skin

- sun exposure
- sugar (see chapter 3 in *What's Age Got to Do with It?*)
- processed foods
- harsh chemicals
- improper cleansing
- saturated and trans fats
- insufficient sleep
- stress
- smoking
- dehydration
- acne

Things That Age Our Bodies

- weak immune system
- disease
- stress
- smoking
- alcohol
- drug use
- inadequate diet/ vitamin and mineral deficiencies
- excess weight
- insufficient sleep

Things That Age Our Overall Appearance

- "old" clothing (that is, clothing meant for someone older than you)
- outdated clothing
- poor posture
- the same things that age our skin and bodies

HOMEWORK

Complete an aging inventory. Take the following "How Am I Aging?" assessment. Please be honest as you take this test.

How Am I Aging?

Place a check in the box next to each statement that is true for you.

	I spend a lot of time in the sun, without sunscreen.
	I eat a lot of sweets and/or processed foods (canned/boxed prepared meals, lunchmeats, etc., particularly those with MSG and/or sodium nitrite/nitrate).
	I wash my face with bar soap.
	I use rubbing alcohol on my skin, as an astringent.
	I go to bed with my makeup on.
	I have acne
	My diet is high in saturated and trans fats.
	I eat a lot of deep-fried foods.
	My job is very high-stress.

	I am suffering a lot of personal stress.
	I am very unhappy and unfulfilled.
	I cry a lot.
	I am a smoker.
	I stay up late and get up early.
	I am sick a lot (colds, flu, etc.).
	I have a diagnosed disease.
	I drink alcohol.
	I drink more than one alcoholic beverage a day.
	I am a drug user.
	I am overweight.

I take a multivitamin every day.	
I eat a balanced diet.	
I exercise at least 30 minutes a day, three times a week or more.	
I stand tall and erect.	
My wardrobe is fashionable and up-to-date.	
I am a happy person, and I laugh a lot.	
I use a good skin care system, day and night.	

I avoid foods with monosodium glutamate and/or sodium nitrite/nitrate.	
I get 8 hours of sleep (or more) a night.	
I drink eight 8-ounce glasses (or more) of water daily.	
I usually or always wear sunscreen during the daylight hours.	
I eat a lot of green, leafy vegetables.	
I eat a lot of whole foods.	
I have at least one bowel movement a day and never have to use laxatives.	
I avoid sweets and excess caffeine.	
I enjoy warm, healthy relationships at home and with friends and coworkers.	
I feel fulfilled in my work and my life (place two checks if you love your job)	
I don't let things "get to me."	
I don't smoke or drink.	
Drugs? Not me!	

Now, examine the results from the "How Am I Aging?" assessment. If your right-hand column is full of checks, congratulations! You will most likely age with grace. You probably already look younger than your same-age friends and acquaintances. But if the majority of checks are in the left-hand column . . . you may want to think carefully about how you really want to look in five, ten, fifteen years. You have already done some damage and are continuing to add years to your appearance—and you may be cutting years from your life.

What's Fitness Got to Do with It?

READING ASSIGNMENT

Chapter 2 from *What's Age Got to Do with It?*

Q: How can exercise help combat the aging process?

A: Studies suggest that regular exercise can reduce your risk of diseases such as heart disease, cancer, diabetes, and osteoporosis; improve cholesterol, blood pressure, insomnia, and depression; and strengthen your immune system, among many other benefits. . . . Because exercise increases circulation throughout the body, it can give your skin a youthful glow.—from *What's Age Got to Do with It?*[1]

Q: Okay, you've convinced me. I need to exercise. But I don't even know where to begin. Can you help?

A: Let me start with a quick review of some tips in *What's Age Got to Do with It?*

Schedule your workouts. Write down or put into your BlackBerry the days and times you plan to work out. This makes it a nonnegotiable event. You'll be less likely to skip it.

Buddy up. Working out with another person often improves the chances that you'll stick with it.

Consult with the experts. Invest in at least a couple of sessions with an expert who can show you proper form and exercises that will help you reach your goals. Or you can talk with friends or family members who are avid exercisers.

Take notes. Write down when you're going to exercise and what you plan to do when you exercise. Then record each workout. How many reps did you do? How long did you exercise? What did you do? How did you feel?

Tell others about your new fitness regimen. Telling others helps you stay accountable. Those who are aware of your get-fit plan will keep you honest.

Set a goal. Whether your goal is losing five pounds, running a 5K race, or just improving your fitness level, having a goal gives you something to strive for. It is also important to have a target date. For example:

"I want to lose 30 pounds by Christmas."

"I want to be a size ____ by my class reunion the weekend of _____."

In addition to long-term goals, set smaller ones too. For example:

"This week, I want to strength train three times."

"Today, I want to run two minutes longer than yesterday."

Q: How can I measure my success?

A: I tend to measure progress by how my clothes fit, but there are some other ways too:

- Use the bathroom scale.
- Take measurements of your body with a tape measure.
- Use an item of clothing regularly to check for body changes.
- Take a basic fitness test at the beginning of your exercise program, to establish your baseline fitness level. (See chapter 2, under "Answers from the Expert," for a list of activities you should complete during this exercise.[2]) The test should be repeated monthly.

Q: How can I get the most from my workouts?

A: By remembering to include both cardio *and* strength train-ing. One of the biggest mistakes women make is concentrating solely on cardio exercises. Cardio burns fat, true, and it's good for the heart, but you also need to provide some form of resistance for your muscles. When you combine cardio and strength training, you will be successful at both chronic calorie burning (calories burned while your body is at rest) and acute calorie burning (calories burned during exercise and for a couple of hours after).

ACTIVITY	CALORIES BURNED PER HALF HOUR*
Bicycling (leisure)	108
Dishwashing	61
Grocery shopping	65
High-impact aerobics	191
Horseback riding (leisurely)	68
Ironing	61
Low-impact aerobics	166
Pilates (beginner level)	101
Running (slow pace)	490
Sex (10 minutes)	38
Vacuuming	79
Walking the dog	107

* Based on a weight of 120 pounds

HOMEWORK

Using your journal, construct a fitness plan that you can make work for you. Start by listing in your journal the days that you can—and will—exercise. What exercises will you do? Will you exercise alone, or with a friend? Where? Be specific. For example, "I will work out alone on Mondays and Wednesdays at home, and with Sally on Tuesdays, at the gym."

Next, take measurements of your bust, hips, waist, and biceps, and write these in your journal. What are your present clothing sizes? Record these too. Then weigh yourself. Jot down your current weight, along with today's date.

Third, write down some goals, both long- and short-term. Remember, this is *your* fitness plan. If it doesn't work for *you*, you'll never stick with it. Don't be afraid to tweak it to make it fit your current physical condition and level of vigor.

Finally, put your fitness plan into action. Using your journal, begin documenting your workouts for the next month. For each kind of exercise you perform, write down how many reps you do. Also record how you feel when your workout is done.

WORKOUT EQUIPMENT AND GEAR

While successful exercise does not require special or expensive gear, there are some items that may be helpful to have:

- ☐ Bathroom scale
- ☐ Stopwatch/timer
- ☐ Heart rate monitor
- ☐ Measuring tape

☐ Dumbbells (5-, 8-, 10-, and 12-pound)

☐ Hand/wrist weights

☐ Ankle weights

☐ Exercise videos/DVDs

☐ Music CDs for aerobic exercise

☐ Good pair of walking/running shoes

☐ Floor mat

☐ Stretching bands

☐ Exercise ball

Q: Besides exercise and a healthy diet, is there any other recommendation you have to help me be the best me that I can be?

A: Yes, there is one *very* critical fitness element that many women never consider: sleep. Most experts say that women need seven to nine hours of restful sleep nightly. Sleep shortened and interrupted by constant wakeups, whether due to anxiety, external factors (such as a howling cat or a crying baby), trips to the bathroom, or night sweats, will not do your body or mind the good that extended, uninterrupted, and body-relaxing sleep will. If you have to hit the snooze button five times in a row before getting out of bed, and you feel as exhausted when you get up as you did when your head hit the pillow the night before, it may be time to start taking some notes and perhaps even speaking to your physician about it.

HOMEWORK

If you believe that your sleep patterns may be adversely affecting your health and life performance, begin recording details about your sleep. For the next week, write in your journal how many hours you slept each night, and between what hours. Then answer these questions: How long did it take you to fall asleep? How many times did you wake up—or get up—during the night? Did you take any naps during the day that may have affected your nighttime slumber? What did you eat during the five hours before bedtime? Did you consume any alcoholic or caffeinated beverages before retiring? What about medications? Were you calm when you went to bed, or depressed? anxious? stressed? What was on your mind that may have had an effect on your ability to sleep peacefully? And when you arose in the morning, how did you feel? Refreshed, or wasted? Did you wake naturally, or by the alarm? The answers to these questions will provide you and your doctor the information you need to help you get the rest your body requires to function at its peak.

What's Nutrition Got to Do with It?

READING ASSIGNMENT

Chapter 3 from *What's Age Got to Do with It?*

Q: What kinds of foods should I eat in order to be healthy?

A: The U.S. Department of Agriculture (USDA) has developed a "Food Guide Pyramid" to help consumers make wise decisions regarding the types of foods they need to eat.[1] Though individuals are meant to customize the pyramid according to their gender, age, height and weight, activity level, etc., the basic plan recommends:

8–11 servings of breads and grains

2–4 servings of fruits

3–5 servings of vegetables

2–3 servings of dairy

2–3 servings of protein

The breads and grains group includes things such as cereals, pasta, rice (preferably brown or wild), bagels, and other sorts of breads, couscous, and so on. Whenever possible, choose whole-wheat or whole-grain versions of these foods.

Eat fruits and vegetables raw as often as possible, and make as many "high-color" selections as you can: bright-red strawberries, bright-yellow peppers, blueberries, and so on. Also, try to eat green, leafy vegetables. Make sure to include cruciferous vegetables in your daily diet (broccoli, cabbage, cauliflower, etc.).

Proteins include dry beans, nuts and seeds, meats and fish, and eggs. Always choose lean cuts of meat, and avoid frying. Nuts are very calorie dense, so be careful how much you eat of them.

The dairy group includes milk, cheese, and yogurt. Go nonfat or low fat whenever possible when eating dairy. Avoid ice cream as much as you can, opting instead for ice milk or low-fat frozen yogurt.

How can you make sure you're getting enough of all the right things? Try this: On the following table, list every item you have eaten today from each food group. Did you come up short at the end of the day? In which column(s)?

Daily Food Groups Consumption Sheet

Bread/ Grains (8–11 servings)	Fruits (2–4 servings)	Vegetables (3–5 servings)	Proteins (2–3 servings)	Dairy (2–3 servings)

HOMEWORK

Using your journal, start recording your food-group consumption so you can get on track with the recommended number of daily servings for each food group. Be aware of any shortfalls in your diet.

STUFF TO AVOID

Sugar/sweets   MSG (monosodium glutamate)

Soda   Sodium nitrite and other nitrates

Imitation sweeteners   Oils, trans fats, saturated fats

Processed foods

Q: What if I need to lose weight? Do I still need to eat all of those servings?

A: Whether you need to lose weight, maintain your current weight, or gain weight, you still need to consume the right amounts of all of the food groups on the pyramid. But if losing weight specifically is one of your goals, you're going to have to cut calories at the same time.

Q: How can I know how many calories are in the foods I eat?

A: Personally, I don't put a lot of emphasis on calorie counting. But if you are interested, there are many excellent tools out there to help women count calories. Supermarket checkout stands abound with various "pocket calorie counters." Bookstores carry larger calorie guides, brand-name calorie counters, and other options. Two very good books are Corinne T. Netzer's *The Complete Book of Food Counts* and *The Calorie King Calorie, Fat, and Carbohydrate Counter* (these also have carbohydrate, protein, cholesterol, fat gram, and sodium counts).[2] The first of these is perfect for your kitchen; the second is just the right size to carry in your purse.

There are also very helpful Web sites, such as www.calorie countercharts.com, which sorts foods alphabetically and lists calories, and www.caloriescount.org, which offers the Calorie Control Council's "Enhanced Calorie Calculator." Just enter a food name in the keyword box and click on the Submit Food Item(s) button to get the number of calories in that food.

Q: I eat out a lot. How can I find the calories in restaurant food?

A: Many books and Web sites feature special sections containing the calorie counts for many popular restaurants, including fast-food chains. Additionally, most major restaurant chains have online nutrition information. One Web site, dietfacts.com, has an extensive list of restaurants that you can choose from. When you click on the restaurant's name, you are given a list of menu offerings. You can get the nutrition facts for any item on the list.

BEST ANTIOXIDANTS

blueberries	cherries	black beans
pomegranates	raspberries	acai berries
cranberries	apples	goji berries

Q: What's your best advice for dieting?

A: As I've said before, "dieting" doesn't work. Instead, you have to commit to a lifestyle that supports day-to-day healthy eating. But if you also want to lose weight, you have to eat the right foods in the right amounts, making sure that you are not consuming more calories than you can burn.

So, how do you know how many calories you need per day? Determining a specific individual's calorie needs can be complex. Factors include age, gender, metabolism, activity level, and so on. But there is a simple formula that can be adjusted up or down for just about any active woman.

Current Weight   _____   (write in your current weight)

           x 12   (multiply your weight times twelve)

       _____   (maintenance calories)

This is the number of calories you need to maintain your current weight. To determine how many calories you should eat if you want to lose weight,

Maintenance calories   _____   (enter the total from above)

          – 500   (subtract 500 from this number)

       _____   (goal calorie count for weight loss)

Based on this formula, use the following chart to determine how many calories you should consume daily.

Weight (lbs.)	Calories Needed to Maintain Weight	Calories Needed to Lose Weight	Calories Needed to Gain Weight
120	1440	940	1940
125	1500	1000	2000
130	1560	1060	2060
135	1620	1120	2120
140	1680	1180	2180
145	1740	1240	2240
150	1800	1300	2300
155	1860	1360	2360
160	1920	1420	2420
165	1980	1480	2480
170	2040	1540	2540
175	2100	1600	2600
180	2160	1660	2660
185	2220	1720	2720
190	2280	1780	2780
195	2340	1840	2840
200	2400	1900	2900

Q: I still need help! I've got to cut pounds—quick!—but I have no idea how to create a low-fat or low-calorie menu!

A: Thankfully, for women just like you, my husband has created a fourteen-day Rapid Start Plan, which was originally published in his book *The Ultimate Weight Solution Food Guide*.[3] You'll find the Rapid Start Plan at the end of chapter 3 in *What's Age Got to Do with It?* The meals listed in that kick-start program are appropriately portioned and nutritionally balanced. By following this healthy food plan for two weeks, you'll get a sense of proper portion size.

If you need more help with weight loss, I recommend that you read Phillip's *Ultimate Weight Solution Food Guide*. There you'll find everything you need to know to learn how to eat for life. In the meantime, here's a sample one-day meal plan to get you started.

Meal Planning Register (sample)

Today I will eat:

Time of Day	Foods	Calories per item	Calories
Breakfast	Black coffee	0	230
	½ papaya, cubed	70	
	poached egg	70	
	1 slice whole-wheat toast with 1 tsp. butter	90	
Midmorning snack	Sliced apple (med.)	80	280
	1 oz. walnuts	200	
Lunch	Turkey sandwich made with 2 oz. white-meat turkey, 2 slices whole-wheat bread, sliced tomato, lettuce, alfalfa sprouts, mustard	260	430
	1 cup grapes	80	
	1 cup skim milk	90	
	green tea	0	

Afternoon snack	Slice of whole-wheat toast with 1 T. honey 135	135
Supper	1 boneless, skinless chicken breast half (approx. 4 oz.), baked or broiled 140 1 baked potato (about 2 inches in diameter) with 2 T. nonfat sour cream 165 salad made with lettuce, sliced green and red pepper, sliced cucumber, and 2 T. vinaigrette 70 cold green tea 0	375
Dinner	1 small container (5.3 oz) Greek yogurt	110

Total calories for the day 1560*

*Note: Any moderately active woman weighing more than 130 pounds will lose weight eating this number of calories

HOMEWORK:

If you want to take charge of your own menu selections, create a meal-plan table for yourself in your journal. Following the example given, plan your meals for a day, or better yet, a week in advance. Remember to make your food choices both healthful and lo-cal.

QUICK TIPS FOR SUCCESSFUL WEIGHT LOSS

- Try not to skip meals. (Especially breakfast!)

- Plan your meals. (Every single one.)

- Keep a food diary. (Don't cheat; your journal won't know, but your hips will.)

- Choose smaller dishes. (The six-inch plate instead of the ten-inch.)

- Make healthy substitutions. (Skim milk, not whole.)

- Read food labels. (Half of that Otis Spunkmeyer muffin, ladies, not the whole thing!)

- Drink enough water. (A minimum of eight 8-ounce glasses a day—more if you work out hard.)

- Flush yourself out. (Eat natural-diuretic fruits and vegetables.)

- Sip green tea. (A natural fat burner.)

- Skip the soda. (It's bad for your bones anyway.)

SUGGESTED SHOPPING LIST FOR EFFECTIVE DIETING

- ☐ bathroom scale
- ☐ tape measure
- ☐ food scale (preferably electronic)
- ☐ calorie book (may also include counts for fat grams, carbs, etc.)
- ☐ measuring spoon set (don't cheat with these!)
- ☐ measuring cup set

SUPPLEMENTS: A RECIPE FOR SUCCESS

Take: 1 multivitamin

Add: A supplement containing 400 milligrams calcium and 400 IU of vitamin D*

Mix with: a high-fiber, low-fat diet heavy in fruits, veggies, and whole grains, plus three glasses of milk or three servings of low-fat yogurt each day . . . for the rest of your life!

Yield: One bone-healthy female

* The recommendation is 1,000 milligrams of calcium and 400–800 IU of vitamin D for women ages 19–49 (which can be obtained easily with the combination of food, dairy, and the supplements listed above) and 1,200 mg of calcium and 800–1,000 IU of vitamin D for women over age 50, according to the National Osteoporosis Foundation.

What's Skin Care Got to Do with It?

READING ASSIGNMENT

Chapter 4 from *What's Age Got to Do with It?*

Q: OK, Robin, you mentioned a lot of good products in chapter 4, and I'd like to try them all. But tell me . . . what do I *really* need in a skin care system? What are the bare essentials?

A: Most skin care systems, at the very least, recommend the use of (1) a cleanser; (2) a "toner" (aka "clarifier," "astringent," etc.); and (3) a moisturizer. But since the skin around the eyes is thinner and breaks down (read "wrinkles") more quickly than your other facial skin, I highly recommend the use of an eye cream too. At the bare minimum, a skin care regimen should include a cleanser, a moisturizer, and an eye cream, day and night.

In saying that, please remember that if you have trouble with breakouts, you will also need to include acne-treatment products in your skin care regimen. If your skin has dry patches, flakiness, or an overall dull appearance, it may require an exfoliating product to slough off dead skin cells. And the most important thing, in any skin care system, is its products' ability to protect your skin from the sun's rays. Check the SPF (skin protection factor) of the products you use. The quicker you burn, the higher the SPF you need. Those who are fairer and burn more easily need SPF 16 or higher. As a general rule, you get about fifteen minutes' protection for each level of SPF: SPF 4 gives an hour's protection; SPF 8, two hours' protection, and so on.

Q: Can I mix and match products from different skin care companies, or should I stick with one brand?

A: I don't recommend mixing brands. Most skin care products are designed to work best in combination with other products in that line. Mixing product lines can result in one product's key ingredient counteracting the active ingredient in another product. You may even experience side effects, such as overdrying, breakouts, or allergic reactions. My advice is to choose a skin care line and stick with it, using products from just that line. Remember to look for products that contain ingredients that stimulate the growth of collagen and protect your skin from sun damage.

SKIN DO'S

- Use sunscreen when you're out in the sun.

- Use a skin care system, day and night.

- Make sure your skin care products contain sun protection (SPF 15 or greater).

- Get your beauty sleep (most women need at least eight hours per night).

- Avoid alcohol.

- Drink plenty of water, and eat water-rich foods.

- Eat lots of fruits and veggies (particularly green leafy vegetables).

- Once a month, examine your skin from head to toe to make sure no moles have changed in size or appearance (possible sign of skin cancer).

- Once a year, if possible, have a professional skin exam. (The American Academy of Dermatology offers free skin cancer screenings nationwide. Visit their Web site at aad.org for more information.)

SKIN DON'TS

Don't smoke.

Don't spend too much time in the sun.

Don't go to bed with your makeup on.

Don't use bar soap (e.g., Zest, Safeguard, Dial) to wash your face.

Don't mix products from different skin care lines.

Q: I have no idea what my skin type is. How can I find out?

A: There are several different ways. One way to find out your skin type is to go by a department store cosmetic counter. A few minutes with a beauty adviser from any of the reputable cosmetic companies (e.g., Lancôme, Estée Lauder, Elizabeth Arden) and you will know your skin type. The beauty experts at any of these counters will ask you a series of questions about your skin. They will use your answers to determine whether you have oily, dry, normal, sensitive, or combination skin. Then, based on your skin type and its unique needs (say, if you have an uneven skin tone, acne, dark circles, eye puffiness, crow's feet, etc.), they can recommend a skin care regimen designed especially for you.

Another way to find out your skin type is to go online. Many companies offer online profiling so you can find out your skin type and obtain a skin care program tailored to that type. (Some don't offer assistance finding out your skin type, but if you already know it, they can match you up with the products that are right for your needs.) Neutrogena's Web site, for example, offers a personal e-Valuation that asks viewers a series of questions and, in the end, suggests products that are right for them. Avon's site also offers help with product selection. The Olay Web site provides tailored skin care routines based on your answers to their interactive Olay for You analysis.

Q: Robin, nearly every product I use burns my skin! Not only that, but I have broken capillaries under my skin, on my cheeks and around my nose. What's wrong with me?

A: You obviously have sensitive skin. You may even be allergic to one of the ingredients in your skin care products. You may need to start using hypoallergenic skin care treatments or even physician's products. Talk to your dermatologist or a beauty adviser—or both—to help you determine the types of products you need and to discuss common allergens in the various skin care products on the market.

HOMEWORK

In your journal, write down the names of any skin care products you'd like to try. If you're uncertain where to start, look through magazines, and make a note of any TV commercials that advertise products that pique your interest. Also, make a list of cosmetic counters you'd like to visit, along with questions you'd like to ask a qualified beauty expert.

Then use these notes as a shopping list when it's time to start making purchases.

If you've used a skin care system before but just weren't diligent about it, start over. For the next week, record your skin care practices in your journal. Which products did you use? How many times a day, and when? At the end of the week, note any improvements that you see. Also make a note of any problems you experienced. Finding the right skin care system for *you* may involve some trial and error. The important thing is that you do find one—and that you use it devotedly.

What's Hormones Got to Do with It?

READING ASSIGNMENT

Chapter 5 from *What's Age Got to Do with It?*

Q: After reading chapter 5, I'm certain that I have a hormone imbalance. How can I be sure?

A: Homework time!

HOMEWORK

Take each of the following self-tests. If you find that you have five or more symptoms from any particular list, I encourage you to see your doctor immediately. Your hormones may indeed be the culprit.

LOW THYROID (HYPOTHYROID DISEASE)

☐ Unexplainable weight gain

☐ Exhaustion, in spite of adequate sleep

☐ Low sex drive

☐ Brittle nails

☐ Under-eye bags

☐ Very high cholesterol, despite healthy diet

☐ A failed Basal Body Test (a number lower than 98 degrees; see chapter 5 in *What's Age Got to Do with It?*)

☐ Difficulty getting up in the morning

☐ Cold hands

☐ Sudden thinning of hair

☐ Frequent inexplicable sweating

☐ Irregular periods

☐ Puffiness of face

☐ Patchy skin

☐ Mysterious drying of skin, with no change in skin care routine

☐ Depression for no reason

☐ Intolerance to cold temperatures

☐ Thinning of eyebrows

SIGNS OF LOW OR IMBALANCED ESTROGEN

- ☐ Difficulty falling asleep
- ☐ Listlessness
- ☐ Forgetfulness
- ☐ Anxiousness
- ☐ Mood swings
- ☐ Premature hot flashes
- ☐ All-day fatigue
- ☐ Loss of stamina
- ☐ Premature night sweats
- ☐ Disinterest in sex
- ☐ Skin dullness
- ☐ Water retention
- ☐ Sagging of breasts
- ☐ Unexplained back pain
- ☐ Pelvic cramps not associated with period
- ☐ Bleeding during intercourse
- ☐ Vaginal itching
- ☐ "Crawling" sensation of skin
- ☐ Frequent yeast infections
- ☐ Stress incontinence (aka "laugh, cough, sneeze" incontinence)
- ☐ Extreme vaginal tightness and subsequent discomfort during sex
- ☐ Breast tenderness
- ☐ Temperature swings coupled with mood swings
- ☐ Loss of the perception of being sensual
- ☐ Migraines
- ☐ An awareness of being "uptight"
- ☐ Sudden nausea

SIGNS OF LOW PROGESTERONE

☐ Missed/infrequent periods

☐ More than one period a month

☐ Excessively heavy periods

☐ Painful breasts

☐ Breasts lumps

☐ Severe PMS

☐ Spotting before period

☐ Cystic breasts

☐ Unexplainable anxiety

☐ Nervousness and irritability

☐ Water retention

☐ Weight change for no apparent reason

☐ Constant fatigue

SIGNS OF LOW TESTOSTERONE

☐ Flabbiness of muscles

☐ Muscle weakness

☐ Loss of energy

☐ Feelings of insecurity

☐ Difficulty with making decisions

☐ Indifference to sex

☐ Loathing of one's body

☐ Loss of pubic and/or underarm hair

SIGNS OF LOW DHEA

☐ Constant feeling of being "stressed"

☐ Loss of stamina

☐ Intolerance for loud noises/music

☐ Nonstop fatigue

☐ Infrequent "good moods"

☐ Frequent colds and overall compromised immune system

☐ Short-term memory loss

☐ Loss of pubic hair

☐ Loss of abdominal muscle tone

☐ Dry eyes

☐ Skin dryness

☐ Loss of interest in sex

SIGNS OF POLYCYSTIC OVARIAN SYNDROME

☐ Hair loss

☐ Development of a "mustache" or other facial hair

☐ Increase in leg and arm hair

☐ Unexplained weight gain

☐ Muscular appearance not resulting from exercise

☐ Onset of acne

☐ Miscarriage

☐ Difficulty in becoming pregnant, even after a first pregnancy

☐ Skin redness

☐ Sudden insulin resistance

Q: What is perimenopause, and what's the difference between it and menopause?

A: Menopause, according to *Merriam-Webster's Collegiate Dictionary*, is "the natural cessation of menstruation."[1] You know that you have reached menopause when it has been one full year since your last period. Perimenopause is the period of time leading up to menopause. During this time you will be noticing changes in your body, the things we discussed in your reading assignment for this chapter: mood swings, vaginal dryness, changes in menstrual flow, etc. This is the season of time that women are talking about when they say, "I'm going through the change."

Q: I may be going through menopause. How can I be sure?

A: Again, if you're going through something, it would be *perimenopause*, not menopause itself (technically, menopause is a one-day event: the day your period stops for good and you never have another). How can you be sure it is perimenopause? Visit your doctor. But before you do, take the "Am I Going Through the Change?" self-test on the next page. It will give you more information to share with your doctor to help him or her determine whether your symptoms are due to perimenopause or something else.

Am I Going Through the Change?

Please read the following statements and place a check next to each statement that applies to you.

- ☐ I am thirty years old or above.
- ☐ I am in my forties.
- ☐ I think I'm having "hot flashes."
- ☐ I wake up soaking in sweat in the middle of the night.
- ☐ I'm hot as a biscuit, even in the dead of winter.
- ☐ I have a hard time getting to sleep.
- ☐ I wake up often during the night.
- ☐ My skin has never been dry, but now it is.
- ☐ I never seem to be interested in sex anymore.
- ☐ Sex is not comfortable for me these days.
- ☐ I have a problem with vaginal dryness.
- ☐ I'm suddenly very moody. No one ever knows what to expect from me.
- ☐ I cry at the drop of the hat for no reason.
- ☐ I've been having heart palpitations recently.
- ☐ My husband says I'm awfully touchy lately.
- ☐ I've always been a happy person, but now I'm depressed a good deal of the time.
- ☐ I can't seem to control my bladder. (Sometimes I leak!)
- ☐ I've been having anxiety attacks.
- ☐ My periods have become extremely heavy. I bleed more than I ever have.
- ☐ I'm hardly having periods at all anymore.
- ☐ My periods have been abnormally light for a long time.

- ☐ My periods are really short these days—one or two days and it's over.
- ☐ I seem to be absent-minded of late.
- ☐ I never got headaches before, but I seem to have them a lot now.
- ☐ Sometimes I skip a period.
- ☐ My kids wonder what's wrong with me. They say I've turned into a grouch.
- ☐ I've never had belly fat, but all of the sudden I have a "jiggly-roll."
- ☐ I'm suddenly getting urinary tract infections.
- ☐ I've become really forgetful recently.
- ☐ I can't seem to concentrate.
- ☐ My breasts are really sore, for no good reason.
- ☐ My face is a mess! I have worse acne now than I ever had as a teenager.
- ☐ Where's all this facial hair coming from?
- ☐ I've put on a lot of weight, really fast—but I haven't changed my eating habits.
- ☐ I could make a wig out of the hair in my brush! It seems like I lose more every day.
- ☐ My nails are so brittle, but they never were before.
- ☐ I've been bloated recently, and I can't explain it.
- ☐ I am so exhausted—and I stay that way, it seems.

If you checked seven statements or more, you may want to see your doctor. If you don't have a doctor, do your homework before going to just any office.

Q: My doctor has told me that I'm definitely perimeno-pausal, but she didn't tell me what to do about it. Is there anything that can make the journey to menopause any easier?

A: Yes! Here's a list of things you should discuss with your doctor that can help you face the challenges that may lie ahead during "the change."

Ask your doctor about:
- ☐ The benefits of acupuncture for perimenopause/ menopause
- ☐ Natural bio-identical hormones (versus synthetic hormones), in particular: estradiol, estriol, estrone, progesterone, DHEA, pregnenolone, and testosterone
- ☐ Homeopathic remedies (e.g., sepia)
- ☐ Physical therapies to help with perimenopausal discomfort
- ☐ Dietary recommendations
- ☐ Recommended supplements (other than those listed below, which you could ask about specifically)
- ☐ Lachesis mutis, glonoinum, and belladonna for hot flashes/perspiration
- ☐ Magnesium and calcium for mood swings
- ☐ Evening primrose oil for mood swings, irritability, breast tenderness, and bloating/water retention
- ☐ L-theanine
- ☐ Things to avoid

You should also network with other women who have gone through what you're going through now. Do you have any friends who have reached menopause? Give them a call to hear how they handled their symptoms, what worked, what didn't, and what doctors or therapies they recommend.

The library and the Internet both offer abundant, valuable resources to help make "the change of life" as seamless as possible. Investigate the various books and Web sites on menopause, but remember: always run everything by your doctor first.

ROBIN'S SHOPPING LIST FOR PERIMENOPAUSAL SYMPTOMS

☐ Fish oil

☐ Evening primrose oil

☐ Magnesium supplement

☐ Calcium supplement

☐ L-theanine supplement

☐ Sepia*

☐ Lachesis mutis*

☐ Glonoinum*

☐ Belladonna*

*Use these only under the care of a homeopathic expert. See *What's Age Got to Do with It?*, **page 125**

Finally, have a talk with your family. Sit them down and explain that you have begun a very natural, normal process, one that will affect how you feel, and perhaps how you act and react. Explain the symptoms you may have. Assure them that it will pass. Most important, get them in your corner. The process of menopause will be so much easier if you have sought your family's support from the get-go.

6

What's Hair
Got to Do with It?

READING ASSIGNMENT

Chapter 6 from *What's Age Got to Do with It?*

Q: I think I need a new hairstyle, but I have no idea where to start. What do I do?

A: First, start with people you know. Whose hairstyles do you simple adore? Take their pictures so you can refer to them later. Next, go through various hair or fashion magazines. Who's wearing a style that you think might work for you? Cut out the photos. Finally, take your photo collection to your salon and talk with a professional stylist. Get his or her opinion on how each style will work with your facial structure, lifestyle, and so on. Is the style high-maintenance, low-maintenance, or no-maintenance? Be sure to take your time into consideration.

Q: What if I don't have a stylist?

A: Simple. Think of people you know personally whose hair you love; then go talk to them, getting salon/stylist names and numbers from each. Or go through the phone book, checking out various salons' yellow pages ads. If that doesn't help you, try searching online for salons in your area, and check out their Web sites. Use your journal to record the contact information so you won't have to look it up later. You can also try visiting TheHairStyler.com. This site allows you to take your facial shape (oval, oblong, square, etc.), hair texture, and hair density into consideration as you try on styles. There are hundreds of styles and colors to choose from, and once you've made some selections, you can learn how to create and maintain the styles you like best. You can save your new look(s) and print them out to take to your stylist. There are probably other Web sites like this one too. Research a few.

Q: I like my style and don't really want to change, but I sure could use a change of color. How do I decide which color is best for me?

A: Start by asking yourself a few questions. First, what do you want from a color? Do you want to totally change shades, or just cover gray? If you're getting a little older, perhaps go a shade or two lighter. If your hair color is just too drab, darken it a shade or two. If you like your natural hair color, but you'd like to "perk it up" a bit, consider some highlights or streaks.

Another thing to consider is how often you want to have to recolor. In other words, how long do you want your color to last? If you're bold, you might choose a permanent hair color, right from the start. If you're hesitant, you may want to choose a color that will be gone within a few shampoos, in case you don't like it. If your life is busy, you may not want to color but once a month, just to touch up your roots.

Next, do you want to be salon dependent, or "you dependent"? Some women are do-it-yourselfers. They would never pay a cosmetologist a higher price when they can do it themselves for much less. But other women are afraid to self-color their hair, or they don't have the time or the patience. In that case, I'd say let the experts manage it.

Finally, how much are you willing to spend, per month, on your hair style and color? If money is no object, go to the salon. If you can't see paying more than thirty dollars for color, do it at home.

NO-NOS FOR LUSCIOUS LOCKS

- Smoking—put down those Virginia Slims, for good!
- Chlorine/salt water—wear a swim cap.
- Extreme heat—apply heat-protective products before drying, and use flat or curling irons on dry hair only.

POWER FOODS FOR TREMENDOUS TRESSES

- Carrots
- Dairy products (remember to choose low-fat products for your cholesterol's sake)
- Dark green (especially leafy) vegetables (e.g., kale, spinach, leaf lettuce, broccoli)
- Eggs
- High-omega-3 fish (especially salmon)
- Legumes (lentils, pinto beans, kidney beans, garbanzos)
- Nuts (especially Brazil nuts)
- Oysters
- Poultry
- Whole grains

Note: If you look carefully, you'll notice that many of these items have something in common. Can you guess? That's right! Protein. That's important, because your hair, ladies, is 98 percent protein.

SHOPPING LIST FOR HAIR PRODUCTS/DEVICES

- Shampoo
- Conditioning rinse
- Leave-in conditioner
- Styling gel
- Styling mousse
- Combs / brushes / picks
- Vent brush
- Round brush
- Blow dryer (with diffuser)
- Curling iron
- Hot rollers
- Spiral curlers / benders
- Flat iron / crimping iron
- Hair spray
- Spray gloss
- Spray-on hair color or highlights (very temporary)
- Brush-on (or smooth-on) temporary highlights
- Clip-on hairpieces
- Hair clips / barrettes and other hair accessories

What's Makeup Got to Do with It?

READING ASSIGNMENT

Chapter 7 from *What's Age Got to Do with It?*

Q: I've never been good at makeup application. I'm not even sure where to start. What should I do?

A: Well, let me start by asking you a few questions. Who can you think of whose makeup always looks flawless? Whose lipstick do you like? Whose eye cosmetics would you like to try? Whose general look would you like to imitate? Write down their names, as well as the products/colors they've told you they use and the companies or salons from which they obtained these products. You can use your list later as a shopping guide. Use your journal to record your friends' names and products. Also list any problems you'd like to correct with makeup or accessories.

You also need to ask yourself if there are any particular problems you'd like to correct, using makeup or accessories. Do you have bushy eyebrows or an eyebrow shape that you don't like? Red, blotchy skin? A sallow skin tone? Acne? Dark under-eye circles? These things will affect your buying decisions.

Q: I have a friend whose makeup is always perfect, but just because those colors look good on her, doesn't mean they'll look good on me. Besides, I've bought products before, but then when I get home, I don't have a clue what to do with them. How can I get help?

A: I recommend, that you visit a cosmetic counter or two. Many cosmetic/skin care shops or department-store cosmetic counters (e.g., Estée Lauder, Prescriptives, Clinique) offer free consultations. Stop by one of these counters and make an appointment (some counters offer on-the-spot makeovers). Their beauty experts will match products to your skin type (oily, dry, combination), tone (fair, light, medium, dark), lifestyle (casual versus high-stress), and desired look (natural, daring, or somewhere in between) and will apply these products to your face. Don't hesitate to ask a lot of questions, and make sure that each beauty adviser who works with you tells you exactly how to duplicate the look he or she created once you walk out of the store.

Another option is to pay to have a professional makeover. Visit a local salon that offers facials and makeovers. If you don't know where to go, look through the yellow pages or online and find a couple of salons whose advertising indicates that they provide cosmetic services. Then make an appointment at one of these salons and see what great look your makeup artist can create. Be sure to tell the artist about any particular "corrective" issues you would like for him or her to address (for example: uneven eyebrows, skin discolorations, small or deep-set eyes, puffy eyelids, or too-thin lips).

In every case, I recommend not buying the mother lode of products right then and there. Whether you've gone to a department store or a high-end salon, wear the products for a whole day, glancing at the mirror from time to time to make sure you like the look every time you see it. (Or ask the makeup artist for samples you can try for a couple of days to make sure there are no issues with allergies, breakouts, and so forth.) It may be an awesome, bold new look that just has to grow on you. Or perhaps you've done bold makeup for years, but a well-trained pro has told you that you need a more natural look or that your appearance is dated. Do your best to listen, but in the end, if you don't like the look, you haven't bought the products. Only buy cosmetics that you intend to use.

Still another option is to go online and visit Web sites that offer virtual makeovers. Taaz.com and DailyMakeover .com are just two of the many sites that allow you to "try on" different colors.

Finally, a variety of books in every price range offer makeup how-tos that can help you get the natural or bold and glamorous look that you want, teaching you everything from how to maximize your eyes to how to hide blemishes, achieve a dramatic night-on-the-town look, or shape the perfect eyebrows.

HOMEWORK

In your journal, make a list of the beauty products you would like to try. Include foundations, blushes, finishing powders, lightening-and-brightening products, *everything* that interests you. For foundation, is your preference a liquid, mineral powder, cream, or liquid-to-powder? For blush, do you want a cream, a powder, or a gel? What about color-correcting products, to tone down yellow skin tone, or to neutralize ruddiness? And don't forget your lips. Do you want to experiment with lip liner? Do you prefer a gloss or a lipstick? Reds, browns, or pinks? There's so much to choose from. Remember to write down both brand names and shades. Eyeliners come in creams, liquids, pencils, and powders; so do eye shadows. Mascara can be wash-off, water-resistant, or absolutely water- and smudge-proof. List everything you want to try, and don't forget the accessories, like sponges, applicator brushes, powder puffs, and so forth. You only have one face. Make it look its best!

What's Fashion Got to Do with It?

READING ASSIGNMENT

Chapter 8 from *What's Age Got to Do with It?*

Q: I know my best colors, and I have a pretty good idea of what styles don't look good on me, but I'm still not sure what kind of clothes would look best on me. I've been through all kinds of fashion magazines, but the information

271

there just confuses me. Sometimes the writers even say conflicting things. I need some help deciding what to put in my wardrobe. Do you have any more suggestions?

A: Yes. Don't ignore the Internet. Search for Web sites that can help you make sound fashion decisions. One good site is My Virtual Model (www.mvm.com). There you can custom create a "model" who looks remarkably like you (same hair color, style, physical dimensions, etc.) and then virtually try on different outfits to find the right look for you. Another site that was easy to find was TryStuffOn.com. There are probably dozens more of these types of sites, and there are even sites for plus-size women. Take advantage of them.

Also, here are some things to keep in mind as you endeavor to make the right fashion choices:

"It is what it is."

Your body is your body, it has its good spots and its bad spots, and you have to choose clothing with its particular shape in mind. If you have broad hips, it does not matter how good your skinny sister looks in that flared skirt or those baggy trousers—you probably shouldn't do it. You may not want to wear clothing that bares a lot of cleavage, if you don't have a lot of cleavage to bare. If you feel that your legs are a bit chunky or perhaps too skinny, don't wear short skirts. Make the most of the body you have. It's your own; it's unique; and you can look beautiful in the skin you're in, by emphasizing the most flattering aspects of your figure. The right clothing selections should always make you look and feel beautiful.

Dress your age.

I'm a firm believer in doing and wearing what I want, and I choose to dress in ways that flatter me and my unique figure, regardless of what is "in" for my age group. I don't like to be told I'm "too old" for this or that. But that said, there are *some* guidelines as to what is appropriate for your particular body at your particular age. The right clothes should look classy and sassy at the same time. So, if you're forty-five, your granddaughter's miniskirt may not be the best pick for you. Stay out of the juniors department! Likewise, if you're twenty-two, you don't want to dress like your great-aunt Aggie (who's seventy-eight and counting). Basically, it all boils down to using simple common sense when you shop.

Don't shop from the runway.

Ever watch one of those fashion shows, where stick-thin models sashay down the runway, looking as if they haven't had a home-cooked meal in ages? Ladies, please understand that what you see on the runway or in *Vogue* is not always meant for day-to-day wear.

It's gotta feel right.

You can look drop-dead gorgeous in that fitted dress, but if it itches or is too tight to breathe, what good is it? You'll be miserable all day. Get clothes that fit your body now, not how it was five years ago or how you hope it will be. They can have a little breathing room, sure. But don't buy an entire wardrobe based on your plan to lose thirty pounds. Buying a wardrobe full of too-tight clothes is nonsensical (not to mention sadistic!). So get clothing, shoes, and undergarments that fit now. (See *What's Age Got to Do with It?* for tips on getting the right bra size.) You can always alter them later, if necessary, or build a wardrobe in your new size, a piece or two at a time, after you've lost (or gained) the weight you planned to.

Q: I recently had a professional clothing profile, and I know what colors and styles are best for me, but now I need to start building a wardrobe. What do I need in my closet first?

A: My recommendations are: (1) a basic black dress, (2) a pair of black slacks in all-weather wool gabardine or a similar fabric, (3) black pumps, (4) a black skirt, (5) a white Oxford shirt, (6) a white silky blouse, and (7) one good pair of jeans. You can add other items—like a blazer, or slacks in gray and white—as you go. But start with these basics, and build from there.

TIPS FOR "TROUBLE SPOTS"

- **Thick waist**: Wear tailored, well-fitted clothing. Choose ruched tops and blazers left unbuttoned, with a camisole or T-shirt underneath. Avoid empire waist tops; sturdy fabrics can disguise less-than-six-pack abs. Dress to show off your best assets (great legs; slender, attractive arms, etc).
- **Flabby upper arms**: Select bell sleeves, three-quarter-length sleeves, or button-down shirts with the sleeves rolled up just above the wrist. Avoid cap sleeves or sleeveless tops.

- **Pear-shaped lower body or large bottom**: Look for dark, boot-cut jeans with big pockets with stitching on them. Wear light-colored or fun, printed tops to bring attention to your upper body; a good, tailored blazer that hits at the hip; and higher-heeled shoes to make your legs look longer. Opt for A-line skirts and dresses to hide a full lower body.

- **Thick calves**: Dark hose or long leggings can slim calves, and for footwear, choose open- or closed-toe pumps. Avoid skintight leather boots and ankle boots.

- **Oversized bustline**: Begin with a minimizing bra. Then choose V-neck or scoop-neck tops or a blouse that's left a little open at the top. Avoid high necklines, closed-neck tops (like turtlenecks), and shirts with lots of ruffles, ruching, or puffed sleeves, as well as heavily embellished or breast-pocketed shirts. Emphasize a slim waist with a belt or a sweater with a banded bottom.

- **Boy-shaped body**: Slim-fitting, tailored tops, and blazers that nip in at the waist can create the illusion of an hourglass figure. Define your waistline with ruched-waist dresses and tops, belts, and wrap dresses. Choose pleated or layered skirts. Avoid straight/pencil skirts.

- **Short frame**: Wear monochromatic clothing to elongate the look of your body. Choose high heels or platforms to add some height. Avoid huge necklaces and extra-large handbags.

What's Faith
Got to Do with It?

READING ASSIGNMENT

Chapter 9 from *What's Age Got to Do with It?*

HOMEWORK

In your journal, write your answers to the following questions:

- What am I doing to create meaning and purpose in my life?

- What role does faith play in my sense of purpose? In my sense of well-being?
- Am I drawing strength from my faith to live my healthiest, happiest life?

If you're not a person of a particular faith, think about why you've made this choice. Should you reconsider and perhaps reengage with a faith to enjoy the full range of being alive and healthy?

Spend some time reflecting on these questions. There are no right or wrong answers here. Just answer each question honestly. This will provide clarity on things that are harder to measure, such as the role of your spiritual life to your life as a whole.

Take as much time and journaling space as you need. The decisions you make regarding faith may be the most important ones of your life.

Notes

Chapter 2: What's Fitness Got to Do with It?

1. Robin McGraw, *What's Age Got to Do with It?* (Nashville: Thomas Nelson, 2008), 17–18.
2. Ibid., 37–38.

Chapter 3: What's Nutrition Got to Do with It?

1. For more information on the Food Pyramid, visit the official USDA Web site at www.mypyramid.gov.
2. Corinne T. Netzer, *The Complete Book of Food Counts*, 8th ed. (New York: Dell, 2008); Allan Borushek, *2008 CalorieKing Calorie, Fat, and Carbohydrate Counter* (Hudsonville, MI: Family Health Publications, 2007).
3. Phil McGraw, *The Ultimate Weight Solution Food Guide* (New York: Pocket, 2003).

Chapter 5: What's Hormones Got to Do with It?

1. *Merriam-Webster's Collegiate Dictionary*, 10th ed. (New York: Merriam-Webster, 1998), s.v. "menopause."

IMPORTANT CAUTION–PLEASE READ THIS